Dr. Isaiah Sessoms

The Black Socio-Cultural Cognitive Learning Style

The Black Socio-Cultural Cognitive Learning Style

Dr. Isaiah Sessoms

ARPress
ILLUMINATING IDEAS
EMPOWERING VOICES

ARPress
45 Dan Road Suite 5
Canton MA 02021

Hotline: 1(888) 821-0229
Fax: 1(508) 545-7580

Ordering Information:
Quantity sales. Special discounts are available on quantity purchases by corporations, associations, and others. For details, contact the publisher at the address above.

Printed in the United States of America.

ISBN-13:	Softcover	979-8-89356-982-7
	Hardcover	979-8-89356-984-1
	eBook	979-8-89356-983-4

Library of Congress Control Number: 2024910594

Contents ━━━━━━━

Dear Participant,

Understanding education and what constitutes a cognitive learning style is, perhaps, the most essential variable in education today. A cognitive learning style represents the essence of an individual and how that individual learns. Children learn from direct experiences in their environment. They learn from role models, by imitating others, by observing others and from the language, written or spoken, in their environment.

Learning is universal. Research on cognition shows that basic learning occurs at similar stages for most children. All children can learn and most children learn to perform basic tasks, such as walking and talking, at relatively the same age. Researchers know that not only is learning universal, but that all children have very distinct preferences of what and how they learn. That is, children make very discriminating choices between what information they will actively commit to memory and what information is discarded. These choices are grounded in their personal life experiences which are indirectly determined by their family, culture and environment.

"Learning is universal....
All children can learn."

Research demonstrates that children alone decide what they want to remember and what they want to forget. As a result of these preferences, children develop, at an early age, their own unique cognitive learning style. This learning style determines their mode of learning. Based on this, children decide and make very conscious choices about learning and whether or not to actively participate in the educational process. This is true regardless of race, culture or socioeconomic background.

The cognitive learning style of an individual is a very precise reflection of the choices and preferences an individual makes and is the core of the learning process. Unfortunately, the public school system ignores cognitive learning styles and inhibits students by placing them in a passive role. Children are expected to learn and absorb information simply because they are told to do so. They are expected to learn regardless of content, emotional readiness to learn, and whether or not they consider this learning relevant in the scope of their life experiences.

Learning requires that very specific and complex cognitive skills be acknowledged before any panacea to the multiple-facet problems facing educators in the public school system: low SAT scores, poor academic performance, high drop out rates, etc... These problems are directly related to the dysfunctional aspects of the public school system which has historically miseducated learning actually takes place. Learning is a cooperative effort between the teacher and the student. Most teachers are familiar with cognition, as presented by Jean Piaget. But most fail to incorporate this important information into their teaching style.

As a result, valuable time is lost in trying to force children to respond appropriately to specific curriculum and classroom activities. When they fail to do so, these children are labeled illiterate, lazy and slow learners.

This handbook was developed to refocus and redirect the attention of teachers and educators to the importance of cognition and cognitive learning styles. It is not meant, however, to be a most of the nation's children.

Too many students leave the public school system unprepared to function in today's highly technological society. Most of these students will be condemned to a life of poverty and want. But understanding cognition is a start. As educators and researchers we realize the very complex problems before us. We know also that most people resist change. Changing the public school system will require the committed efforts of teachers, administrators, parents and students and this task will not be easy.

In presenting this handbook we ask only that you approach this effort with optimism and objectivity. After all, we have nothing to lose and absolutely everything to gain if we can make teaching Black students easier and more enjoyable for even one teacher.

> Dr. Isaiah Sessoms
> Executive Director
> Educational & Social Research

Section I

Introduction

The Melting Pot Theory, popular at the turn of the century, resulted in the hypothetical lumping together of all ethnic groups in America. The idea was that through the process of assimilation and acculturation everyone would embrace and emulate the values and beliefs of White America. This social theme was reflected in the philosophy of the public school system. Traditionally, education in the United States was developed to perpetuate the values, beliefs, traditions, customs, folkways, morals, language and perspectives of the dominant group - white America. To make this work, however, a number of assumptions had to be made about learning:

1. *All children, regardless of race and culture learn in precisely the same manner, and,*
2. *Variables such as culture and racial identity were considered insignificant components in the learning process.*

Although both of these assumptions were incorrect, they provided the basic foundation for the social climate of the school system. Thus, the public school focused on indoctrinating all of its students into the beliefs, values, customs and traditions of white mainstream America and chose to ignore the culture, ethnicity, or religious affiliation of its nonwhite students.

The culture of white Europeans was considered and treated as superior to all other cultures and was used as standards by which to measure the academic ability and achievement of its nonwhites pupils. These same assumptions were reflected in the attitudes of educators toward nonwhite students served by this school system. Unfortunately, this ethnocentric approach to education resulted in the gross mis-education of thousands of ethnically different children. Not only were these children required to embrace, copy and, thus, emulate the values and beliefs of White America,

1

they were graded and evaluated on how well they conformed to these standards and beliefs.

This approach was harmful in other ways too. Research in Cognition shows that various features of the cognitive learning style of children emerges from the stimuli present in three areas: family, culture and environment. For years most of the curriculum used in the public school system depicted the culture, family and environment of ethnic minorities as inferior, undesirable, and substandard. Very little has changed. Today, most multi-culture materials used in classrooms are still presented as supplemental materials or handouts. The primary curriculum remains the same. Ethnicity is doled out in increments: Black History Month and Cinco De Mio. The remainder of the year white history is taught.

Unfortunately, the public school system has historically negated the culture, lifestyle, values, beliefs, traditions and language of nonwhites. This practice has resulted in very significant aspects of the learning process being lost. This benign neglect fosters a negative learning environment in which learning is impossible for nonwhites children. The end result is that the majority of these children will not learn, nor will they become productive, active members of the society.

Statistics show that by the year 2000, 88% of the nation's teachers in the public school system will be white, while almost 60% of the student population in these schools will be ethnic minorities. If educators hope to produce productive, contributing citizens, then changes in the way we teach nonwhite children are not only necessary, they are vital to the total society.

In effect, teachers must become more committed to the idea of cultural diversity. Understanding the cognitive learning style of Black children which is based, primarily, on the life experiences within the context of family, culture and environment, is a start in that direction.

****

OVERVIEW OF HANDBOOK ———————————

This handbook is designed to assist teachers to utilize information pertaining to the Black Socio-Cultural Cognitive Learning Style in their teaching assignments. Research shows I that the academic performance of students improve significantly if teachers focus on the learning style preference of the students.

Specific observational assessment tools have been developed for this Handbook to provide teachers and educators with the practice needed to effectively use information pertaining to the Black Socio-Cultural Cognitive Learning Style. One aspect of this workshop will be to teach educators how to properly assess the positive strengths of Black students. This approach enhances the skills teachers and educators need to work effectively with Black students.

In addition, the Handbook includes not only an introduction to the Black Socio-Cultural Cognitive Learning Style, but also methods, techniques and strategies on putting this information to use in the classroom.

Major objectives of this handbook are:

1. **Learn how to Identify Learning Preferences and Strengths of Black Students.**

   a. To train teachers on how to effectively teach to the learning style of Black Students.
   b. To train teachers on how to identify techniques to support and encourage Black students to learn.
   c. To train teachers on how to teach more effectively in a multi-culture classroom environment.

2. **Explore Techniques to Enhance the Learning Experience**

   a. Train teachers how to identify variables essential to the academic success of African American students.
   b. Train teachers to develop teaching curriculum to enhance the learning experience of African American students.

    c.   Train teachers to identify skills which will enhance teaching methods aimed at sociocultural learning.

    d.   Train teachers to explore the Black Socio-Cultural Cognitive Learning Style, using a Teaching-Observational instrument.

3. **Learn New Teaching Concepts**

    a.   Train teachers about learning styles/instructional styles.

    b.   Train teachers to explore research on the Black Socio-Cultural Cognitive Learning Style.

    c.   Train teachers to observe and practice techniques using variables identified in the Black Socio-Cultural Cognitive Learning Style to develop lesson plans.

The Handbook will present alternatives for working with African American students. It is our major objective to assist teachers in acquiring comprehensive techniques, strategies, knowledge and methods that can be applied to everyday teaching situations. We all know that one of the most crucial problems in education today is effectively teaching urban area children. The Black Socio-Cultural Cognitive Learning Style will fine-tune your teaching skills and abilities.

****

Section II

Theoretical Construct: The Black Socio-Cultural Cognitive Learning Style

Premise: Effective learning for Black children has its origin in three dimensional levels

    a. Family
    b. Culture
    c. Social Environment

These three elements form the basis of the Black Socio-Cultural Cognitive Learning Style. Research shows that these three elements are interrelated and that learning is the result of interaction within the social/cultural context of the environment, based on:

1. Cultural Relativity which provides the core of a meaningful learning experience.
2. Family Orientation which provides the stimulus for conceptual formation in learning.
3. Environmental Equilibrium which serves as the catalyst of social learning

These three components form and shape the perception of Black children and these perceptions serve as the channel through which all learning takes place.

Defined, The Black Socio-Cultural Cognitive Learning Style is the way Black children perceive, react and learn as a direct result of the impact of family, culture and environment. These variables are interrelated, each plays a critical role in the total social, cultural and cognitive development of Black children. Eight distinct features emerge out of the Black life-experience of family, culture and environment. These eight features form the nucleus of the Black Socio-Cultural Cognitive Learning Style.

Dr. Isaiah Sessoms (1975)

5

THE SIGNIFICANCE OF FAMILY, CULTURE AND ENVIRONMENT ON THE COGNITIVE LEARNING STYLE OF BLACK CHILDREN

FAMILY

The family is the major force in the shaping of a Black child's social outlook, well-being and socio-cultural cognitive learning style. Most Black children, especially those growing up in large urban areas, grow up in an extended family environment. The structure of the family determines values, beliefs, language, behavior, social conditioning, sense of self, kinship ties, role models, loyalty, motivation, self-esteem and self-image. It is from within the structure of the family that the socio-cultural personality of young Black children develop in the formative years.

The family is also the prime agent of social conditioning of children within the home. It is from the family that children learn how and what to value. Values play a paramount role in the life of children by providing needed guidance and direction. Children acquire values through the process of socialization provided by their family. There has been considerable debate in recent years on the breakdown of the Black family, especially in America's inner cities. These families have been described as dysfunctional, inferior and void of any positive attributes. Black children have been described as being uncared for, unloved and neglected. To be sure, the emergence of drugs in the form of crack cocaine in Black communities nationwide has taken a devastating toll on Black families in the inner cities. But drugs are not confined to the inner cities. Statistics show that 60% of drug use is in the suburbs. Public officials have knowingly adopted a "blame the victim" attitude towards families and children of these families in the inner cities.

The white controlled media has historically projected an image of drug use as being synonymous with being Black, in the same manner they have projected an image the primary welfare recipients as being Black. 60% of those receiving welfare are white. However, because of deeply embedded racism, which prevails in American society, it is politically correct and expedient to continue to develop and perpetuate negative images of African

Americans and other nonwhite minorities. These myths are needed to reinforce racist stereotypes about Blacks and preserve the myth of racial superiority of whites.

It is estimated that by the year 2000, more than 60% of children served by the nation's public schools will be nonwhite, while 80% of teachers will be white. It would be naive to think that white teachers, who are culturally unaware, can effectively teach nonwhite children. Educators have to reconcile themselves with this incredibly lopsided approach to education and be willing to implement desperately needed changes. Working with inner city children who are exposed to drugs, crime and poverty presents a unique challenge for educators. These children are not inferior. They are no different than white children and they deserve the chance to develop their cognitive potential. By continuing to accept racist explanations of the academic ability of African Americans as suggested in Charles Murray's seriously flawed "Bell Curve" theory, public school officials run the risk of relegating another generation of inner city youths to poverty and despair. Thus, we are doomed to repeat this continual history of failure. According to Ray Risk: Children who are perceived as uneducable begin, eventually, to act out this perception and become uneducable.

CULTURE

Cultural diversity has always been a dramatic aspect of American life. For many centuries social scientist acknowledged only the dominant culture of white Americans. Blacks were said to be "cultureless." The notion that Americans had only one culture - the American culture, shamelessly denied nonwhite Americans their right to their cultural identity. When it became popular to admit that other cultures existed after the cultural revolution of the sixties, it was too late. The standards, rationale and objectives of the public school system had already been established. Today all nonwhite students are expected to adapt and conform to these standards manifested in the ideology of the dominant white culture.

African Americans have a very distinct culture - so does Asian Americans, Native Americans, Hispanics and Southeast Asian Americans. These cultures are decisively different from the dominant white culture. The fact that African Americans have a different culture does not mean that African

American culture is inferior to the dominant white culture. It means, simply, that how African Americans view the world, what they value, how they relate, what they believe and love, is entirely different from the way white Americans view and react to the same world.

A good example of this is the Texaco fiasco in which Blacks were referred to as "Black Jelly Beans." This did not come as a surprise to most Blacks who have a pretty good idea of what really goes on in the nation's board rooms. Is it possible that whites think Blacks can't see or understand racial disparity in the work force? Do whites really believe that Blacks think whites are economically successful because of merit? Or that more Blacks are imprisoned because Blacks are more criminal? With few exceptions, Blacks know the devastating impact of racism in America. The recent OJ Simpson trial clearly illustrates how clearly Blacks understand racism. More than any single act in the last decade, this trial showed the world the reality of racially polarization in American society and how deeply racism shapes the mentality of white Americans. More than anything else the trial pulled the cloak oft of white racism. African Americans didn't learn anything new from the trial, but the rest of the world, which is 80% nonwhite, did.

If anything, the trial showed how significant culture is in this society. Not only is culture important in the criminal justice system, research shows that culture is very important in terms of learning. From culture children learn how to view society and perceive and react to the world around them. Culture determines: cultural values, customs, traditions, group identity, habits, cultural norms, images, political expression, social organization, language, group interaction and aesthetic views and beliefs.

For nonwhite children, whose culture has been minimized and negated, cultural conflict and cultural imbalance is inevitable. Piaget referred to this as "equilibrium imbalance," which must be resolved successfully before learning can take place. How well African American children and other nonwhite children are able to adapt and conform to the dominant culture, determines how well they will achieve academically. Those who do not do well are usually viewed by their white teachers as being intellectually and socially inferior and suffering from some type of cognitive deficit.

Educators must be willing to reexamine the way children learn and incorporate into the educational process a value free/culture free zone that is all encompassing of all cultures. By becoming more accepting and tolerant of other cultures, educators and teachers will be able to bridge the gap between teaching and learning.

<u>ENVIRONMENT</u>

The role of environment helps to reinforce the impact of family and culture in the total socio-cultural development of young African American children. It also helps to determine role identity, life experiences, self-reality, a global view of self and others, the role of the significant others, role models and the child's place in the world. Just as there are differences in cultures between Blacks and whites, there are also differences in environment. These differences, however, are the direct results of social circumstances which are rooted in the inequitable economic structure of society. Statistics show that more than 50% of all African American families live below the established poverty level and that only a small percent of African American families have reached the status of middle class.

Economics determines lifestyle, mental and physical health, attitudes, behavior, values, belief systems, psychological well being and even the self-image of an individual. In this society we are taught that an individual's worth is based on his or her economic status. We all know that this is not true. However, because much of what we know about each other is based on myths and stereotypes, it is assumed by many that the environment of most African American families is deprived, impoverished and lacking the type of qualities essential to a healthy, enriched environment.

What most researchers don't understand about African American culture is that although a large percentage of African American families are faced with incredible economic hardships, these families are still able to maintain and provide their children with culturally enriched environments. Historically, African American have learned to adapt to the lopsided structure of the society. This adaptability is reflected in all aspects of the lifestyle of most African Americans: food, housing, forms of entertainment, attitudes, behavior and even in child rearing practices.

How African Americans view the world, their window of reality and how they function in the broader white society, emerges from and is directly related to this cultural environment which is distinctly Black. African American parents still want for their children all of the social and economic rewards the society has to offer. However, how African Americans go about achieving the worthwhile aspects of the American dream is one of the qualities which distinguishes African American from whites, whether it involves purchasing expensive clothes for their children or driving an expensive car. This behavior is a visual response to racial oppression and a direct response to American racism which says that in spite of the oppression and discrimination the good life is not necessarily a white social endeavor. For the most part, the majority of African Americans are hard-working, honest, tax paying citizens who try to raise decent children. All African Americans can identify, understand and interpret racism and racist behavior. This is what they teach their children.

It is critical that educators understand African American culture and the environment from which most African Americans come in order to purge historical and racist misconceptions that African American culture is impoverished and worthless. It is equally critical that school officials and educators modify their view of African American families and stop assigning negative qualities to the type of environment African Americans experience. Whites can not afford to assume that enriched cultural environment is a particular characteristic of the white culture, anymore than they can afford to assume that the prime determinant of an enriched environment is money. Instead, whites and African Americans must realize that the unique and creative cultural environment of African Americans has emerged as a result of a host of historical variables and is not inferior to white culture - but only decisively different from an environmental perspective.

****

PRINCIPLES OF THE BLACK SOCIO-CULTURAL COGNITIVE LEARNING STYLE

The Black Socio-Cultural Cognitive Learning Style Matrix is designed to assist teachers, administrators, students and parents in understanding the socio-cultural strengths which Black students bring with them into the teaching situation. This information will assist educators in developing competence in applying learning style information effectively in the teaching/learning situation and aid Black students in realizing their educational potential.

PRINCIPLES

1. The Matrix focuses on eight distinct variables which comprise the Black Socio-Cultural Cognitive Learning Style.
2. Implementing the style will assist teachers in identifying the socio-cultural strengths of Black students.
3. This information will assist teachers in developing competency skills in teaching Black students effectively.
4. This information will assist teachers in developing strategies to enhance the learning environment of Black students in all disciplines.
5. Information on the model will equip teachers with a reservoir of strategies to use in teaching Black students.
6. The information on the Black Socio-Cultural Cognitive Learning Style will assist teachers in developing educational alternatives to utilize when teaching Black students.

REVIEW OF THE MATRIX DEVELOPMENT MODEL OF THE BLACK SOCIO-CULTURAL COGNITIVE LEARNING STYLE

Cognitive development patterns of children have been the focus of research by many leading psychologists and educators for a number of years. Jean Piaget, a leading authority in the field of cognition, hypothesized that cognitive development occurs as a result of the child's understanding, inferences, abstractions, logical rules and problem solving ability. According to Piaget, cognition develops entirely as a result of unsatisfactory interaction of children in their environment. This hypothesis has been used as the criteria by many educators to develop and design curriculum and teaching strategies. It has also been used as a measurement of academic achievement.

Since cognition develops as a result of interaction in the environment of children, it is safe to assume that environmental factors have a significant impact on the process of cognitive development. Some of the most important aspects of the environment are family and culture. Moreover, if these factors vary from culture to culture, and they do, then it is reasonable to expect that the cognitive development patterns of children would depend on their culture group affiliation. In addition, research demonstrates that environmental encounters permit the learning of necessary component skills: perception, motor development, linguistic and social skills. Since these encounters are different as a result of group membership, it is reasonable to expect that societal values would also be different and would impact the relevance of these acquired skills for both student and teachers in a multi-culture society.

Simply put - ***Black children learn differently.*** As a result, for these children the learning process is different. For example, Black children place more relevance on certain types of material precisely because the environmental factors which impact their lives are different, from the environmental factors which impact the lives of children from mainstream America. It is these differences which are at the core of the Black Socio-Cultural Cognitive Learning Style. The **Matrix Development Model** of the Black

Socio-Cultural Cognitive Learning Style illustrates eight distinct features found within the framework of the family, culture and environment of Black children which directly impacts the socio-cultural cognitive learning style of these children. These features are outlined in the following table.

1. Extended family structure
2. Cultural resiliency
3. Cultural creativity
4. Early maturation
5. Group orientation
6. Environmental autonomy
7. Expanded language pattern (Bio-dialectic)
8. Highly developed motor skills

1. EXTENDED FAMILY STRUCTURE: The majority of Black children growing up today are most likely to live in an extended family situation. That is, families which include uncles, aunts, other relatives and even close family friends. This type of family arrangement is usually the results of economic necessity which has plagued Black communities nationwide since the end of the Civil War.

Growing up in an extended family, however, is a very positive experience. The extended family environment is very enriching and cultivates and promotes close kinship ties. This family arrangement fosters feelings of cooperation versus competition; mutual trust versus dependency. It also provides the child with numerous role models and strong group and family identity. Researchers in cognition know that cognitive growth involves personal interaction and context (Rebok, et al, 1988). Living in an extended family encourages personal growth through active interaction. It also broadens personal perspectives and interpersonal skills. Piaget (et al), suggest in their research that young children learn by observing others in their environment.

This observational learning is enhanced in the extended family arrangement just because there are, obviously, more people to observe and more opportunities to interact with others. In addition, the extended family environment fosters strong cognitive skills such as the ability to differentiate, make choices and decisions. Black children are not only required to differentiate between people, but between situations and circumstances as well.

From within the framework of the extended family, Black children learn very early in life a concept of self in relation to others, knowledge about others, social perspective and role-taking within the family. Researchers in cognition identify these types of experiences as key to wholesome cognitive development.

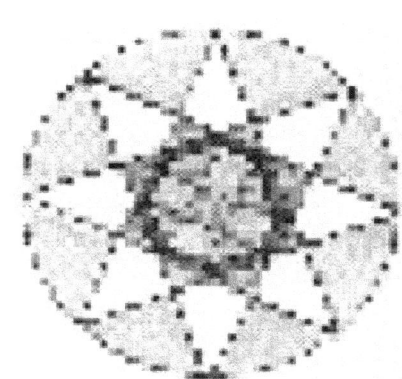

2. CULTURAL RESILIENCY: Cultural resiliency is the ability of a cultural group to withstand vigorous attacks on its culture, lifestyle, values, norms, traditions, beliefs and group identity by other ethnic groups. Race and racial identity has historically played a major role in the American psyche. Cultural resiliency has enabled Black children to maintain their cultural identity in the midst of a public school system which was designed to perpetuate the norms and values of White America and negate the worth and dignity other ethnic groups.

Black children are bombarded everyday with various psychological events and situations which impact their lives and sense of well-being. Value conflict, self-awareness, racial identity, self esteem and self image are ever present threats to cultural identity with the demands being placed on them to assimilate and adapt to the norms and values reflected in the public school system. In addition to having to learn the curriculum and adjust to others in the classroom environment, Black children are also faced with the problem of classifying and organizing issues regarding race and their role in the external world.

Studies show that children are aware of race and all its implications as early as age three (Kenneth Clark, et al). Black children see from their window of reality a conflicting reality - a reality that is sharply different from their own. Images that they see are drastically different from images they encounter in their own environment; people they see in authority are white; people on television, people displaying financial wealth, teachers and administrators - are usually white. Cultural resiliency is the ability of young Black children to maintain their psychological equilibrium in the face of these conflicting cultural images.

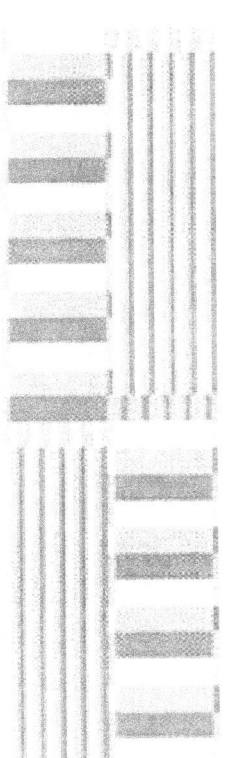

3. **<u>CULTURAL CREATIVITY</u>**: Creativity is not a quality exclusive to American's middle class. Black children are highly creative. Unfortunately, this quality is often overlooked and ignored in a school atmosphere which puts Black children on hold until they drop out of school. According to researchers in the field of cognition, creativity is an indicator of highly developed cognitive skills. Piaget (et al) believed that creativity and play enhances various cognitive skills such as language development and problem solving skills.

Black children are very creative in their environment in spite of the fact that the majority of Black families can not afford to provide these children with expensive playthings. In response to this scarcity, Black children learn to improvise and create their own sources of amusement. The ability to improvise and create play with limited resources is not only a definite cognitive strength, but it also reflects highly sophisticated cognitive skills. For Black children creativity takes the form of dancing, humor, joking, role playing, word play, sports, teasing, jumping and group games that require no objects which have to be purchased: Kick-the-can, jump rope, stick ball, etc... These are common street games in urban areas. All of these activities involve highly complex cognitive responses. Music and dancing, for example, is a significant aspect of the Black culture. Both are used in play, social and religious events. Not all Black children can dance and sing, but most will try to participate. To most young Black children dancing is a cultural expression of play that requires participation and involvement. It is learned by observing others, by memorizing complex moves and rhythms and being able to recall, retain and transfer information rapidly.

Translated in cognitive terms, this intense involvement and participation in play involves a host of complex cognitive skills: memorization, transfer of information, recall ability, analytical skills, evaluation and assessment ability, the ability to identify visual cues and motivation. It also requires decision-making and problem-solving skills. From music, dancing and play Black children learn how to negotiate and how to interact with others. More importantly, they learn about themselves and experience a sense of autonomy while acquiring a sense of fair play. These are positive cognitive strengths that have historically been ignored in the public school system.

4. **EARLY MATURATION**: As a result of severe economic deprivation and poverty, many Black children grow up in single-parent households, or in households in which both parents work. This requires that young Black children take on a more mature role within the structure of the family. Role expansion might include taking care of younger siblings, trips to the store, cleaning and taking on additional household duties in the absence of the parents.

Thus, taking care of younger children, running the household in the absence of parents and other added responsibilities are normal functions in the growing up process of young Black children. Moreover, this role expansion becomes more complex with age as additional responsibilities are added.

From a cognitive perspective, some theorists believe that cognitive growth is the result of the gradual accumulation of various behaviors shaped by experiences. For Black children, these early experiences results in the learning of complex cognitive skills: understanding sequences of responsibilities, both motor and verbal; highly developed interpersonal skills, maturation of sensory receptors and neurological development. All of these skills heighten and enhance cognitive development and growth.

Within the framework of the family, Black children are viewed as essential, contributing members of the household. However, the focus is not on reading, writing and math. Rather, the focus is on cooperation, sharing, participation, contributing and collective behavior. Overall, Black children are active, participating members of their families. These are essential qualities of cognitive development.

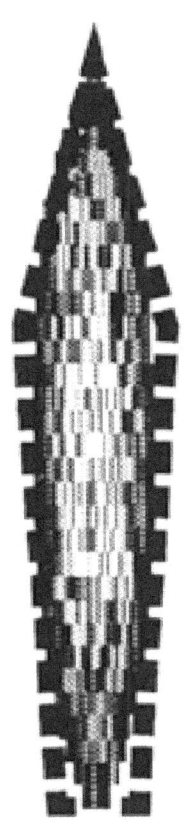

5. **GROUP ORIENTATION**: All ethnic groups in society strive to preserve their group and maintain group interests. As part of the innate drive to maintain a sense of group identity and to survive, all groups opt to their best interest. Blacks are no different in this respect. Black children are born into a distinct, socio-culture group that has historical roots, cultural identity and values. For Black children, their culture is their birth right.

During the formative years, Black children learn about their culture, their identity and their role as a member of the culture from others in their environment, part of the socialization process involves indoctrinating children into the values, norms, beliefs and traditions of the group. This is done, usually through behavior which the children observe and imitate. Most Blacks develop close in-group ties as a result of generations of racial discrimination and oppression. Cultural resiliency among Blacks serve as a buffer against the external environment outside of the group which many Blacks view as hostile. Black children learn about oppression from others within their environment. From this information they develop a concrete, even unique, perspective about the world around them.

However, as a result of this, Black children learn very young to be very analytical. They use this skill to develop major strategies to use in their encounters with the outside world. Their behavior, reaction and interaction in this outside world is viewed in a cultural context. This same type of group orientation also enables Black children to identify similarities and differences between those in their environment and those in the outside world. They learn how to draw conclusions and how to interact on the information they glean from their environment. And, they respond to this information in a cultural context.

Black children learn very young to make clear distinctions between ethnic groups, social status and assigned social roles. From a cognitive perspective this heightened personal interaction is an essential aspect of cognitive growth. The ability to make choices, discern information, differentiate, assign value, make distinctions, develop strategies and to act on information presented represents highly developed cognitive skills. As a result of their group orientation, Black children acquire these skills very early in life.

 **6. ENVIRONMENTAL AUTONOMY:** Social cognition is defined as the ability of the child to understand feelings, thoughts and intentions of the self (self knowledge) and others (role taking) Role taking is the ability to assume the perspective of others and to understand their feelings and thoughts. This definition is important in understanding what is meant by environmental autonomy which most Black children growing up in large urban areas experience very early in life. As a member of the urban Black family, Black children learn to function at different social levels and, as a result, experience a strong sense of autonomy. In the family and at play, Black children learn to be independent very early in life.

A diverse neighborhood and the extended family environment provides for Black children a broader environment that encourages a sense of identity based on territory and space. From this Black children learn to interact in their environment. They learn to develop priorities, screen sensory stimuli, make distinctions between people, identify allies, develop highly diverse peer relationships and interpersonal skills. This enhances the child's sense of self in relation to his or her internal and external environment.

1. Physical self which is behavior related to physical abilities (movement, skills, etc).
2. Active self which is behavior which influences people.
3. Social self which is behavior based on the approval or disapproval of others, and
4. The psychological self which is behavior that includes learned skills and motivation.

18

As a result of their environment, Black children learn to make rapid decisions and react quickly to fast changing visual cues they receive from others in their environment. They are able to adapt quickly to environmental changes, demands and existing realities. This behavior has resulted in some researchers suggesting that Black children need immediate gratification. This is not true.

Black children are very flexible and very tolerant of others in their environment. They learn very early in life to embrace diversity and view differences as a normal part of their environment. These qualities are very essential to cognitive growth and development.

7. BIO-DIALECTIC LANGUAGE PATTERNS (BILINGUAL): Language is a very important part of human development primarily because language reflects the essence of culture. Language historically defines cultural aspects of human societies. According to researchers in cognition, language ability in children develop approximately around the same age. Language is viewed as subordinate to cognition primarily because knowledge can be represented in various forms, both linguistically and non-linguistically. However, although language represents only one aspect of expression of thought, it is a very important aspect of human identity. It represents the totality of the individual and the culture to which that individual belongs.

In the public school system, however, language is an intricate part of the learning process. Children are taught to speak, read and write what has come to be known as "Formal English". The majority of Black children are bilingual. That is, they speak a language that is a product of their culture. There has been considerable research regarding the impact of "Black English", as a dialect, in the context of learning.

For years Black English was considered by many researchers to be incorrect and lacking in positive cognitive quality. African American children were usually penalized for speaking Black English. More importantly, they were, and continue to be, compared to white students. Teachers, unaware of the significance of language, would grade students on how well they speak formal English. Most teachers believe that Black English is inferior to standard English and grade their students accordingly. Consequently, because African American students speak differently, they usually perform poorly in English classes in which the only acceptable language pattern is standard English.

Recent research in the area of language and cognition suggest that African Americans are bilingual and speak a language which differs sharply from what has come to be known as standard English. More importantly, Black English, as it has been called, has been shown to be as relevant and sophisticated as standard English and not inferior. William Labov (1970) suggested that although Black English is very distinct, it is not deficient. It has its own complex language structure and logical rules. African American children develop a Bio-dialectic language pattern precisely because they are members of the African American culture. This language pattern is not inferior and involves a mixture of standard and Black English. African Americans use this language in their primary internal environment, such as the home and the community, and sometimes, in school.

Formal English, on the other hand, is based on a white European dialect and has been identified as the national language to be taught in the public school system in this society. Not only has this language been designated as the official language, all other language patterns are deemed improper, substandard and, sometimes, inferior. Being Bilingual has had a tremendous impact on how Black children absorb information. First, they must assimilate data, translate this information, assess and analyze its relevance and then respond by reversing the order of this process.

Thus, being bio-dialectic requires greater verbal productivity. Houston (1970) showed that Black children employ two different modes of communication. One he labels a "school register," which Black children use in their interaction with teachers and school officials. The other he labels a "non-school register," which these children use in their interaction with their friends and family.

This bio-dialectic language pattern African Americans exhibit involves hearing, storing, remembering, transferring, reasoning, encoding, recalling and assimilating data rapidly. This process requires highly develop cognitive skills in terms of language development. This same language pattern consist of a mixture of descriptive nouns, adjectives and adverbs, shorten phrases and expressions which serve Black children both in and out of their environment. Semantically, being bio-dialectic requires that Black children be selective and attentive when listening to oral instructions. How well and accurately they are able to translate standard English into Black English will depend on how well they listen. More importantly, Black English is an intricate, vital aspect of the Black culture that involves important cognitive processes.

8. **<u>HIGHLY DEVELOPED MOTOR SKILLS</u>**: Learning to use their physical self is an intricate aspect of the cognitive development of Black children. Movement and physical involvement used in various activities in the home and at school is a dominant characteristic of most Black children. Being able to perform highly complex motor activities is the direct result of a highly developed cognitive process.

Motor skills are produced from cues or stimuli from within the environment and involves an elaborate cognitive process. Executing complex motor tasks involves: short and long term memory, imagery, problem-solving ability, thinking, perception, use of past knowledge and information, listening, properly assessing visual cues, retention and retrieval capabilities, giving and interpreting feedback, analytical ability, physical agility, a deliberate use of certain conscious control process and an ability to execute a series of commands. Intense concentration is also involved.

All of these skills are valuable cognitive skills and are valuable clues to the academic ability of Black children. Singer & Gerson (1955) identifies a number of cognitive activities involved in the performance of highly developed motor skills:

1. Converting instruction information
2. Analyzing relationships
3. Retrieving information
4. Understanding task goals
5. Selecting cues
6. Establishing personal goals and expectations
7. Concentration
8. Maintaining optimal arousal (motivational) state
9. Analyzing the nature of the task
10. Mentally rehearsing prior to and/or after performance
11. Adapting to stress
12. Analyzing outcomes of decisions
13. Making correct response decisions
14. Conserving energy
15. Evaluating on going performance when appropriate and possible
16. Evaluating the results of performance (feedback)
17. Attributing performance outcomes objectively

In addition, highly developed motor skills involves the ability of the child to self-generate information. These skills involve situational determined learning and are a conscious activity that a learner used to organize, regulate, receive and transmit information to illicit desired motor behavior. This requires organizational and decision making abilities.

Most Black children can perform highly complex dances. Most demonstrate excellent physical abilities. Research has shown that these skills are evidence of cognitive strengths which can be used in other cognitive activities. Highly developed motor skills demonstrates that Black children are motivated, able to concentrate quite well and have good memories. These skills require encoding, feedback, retention, recall abilities, analytical abilities, the ability to retrieve information and strong decision-making abilities.

****

CONCEPTUAL MODEL THE MATRIX MODEL OF THE BLACK SOCIO-CULTURAL COGNITIVE LEARNING STYLE

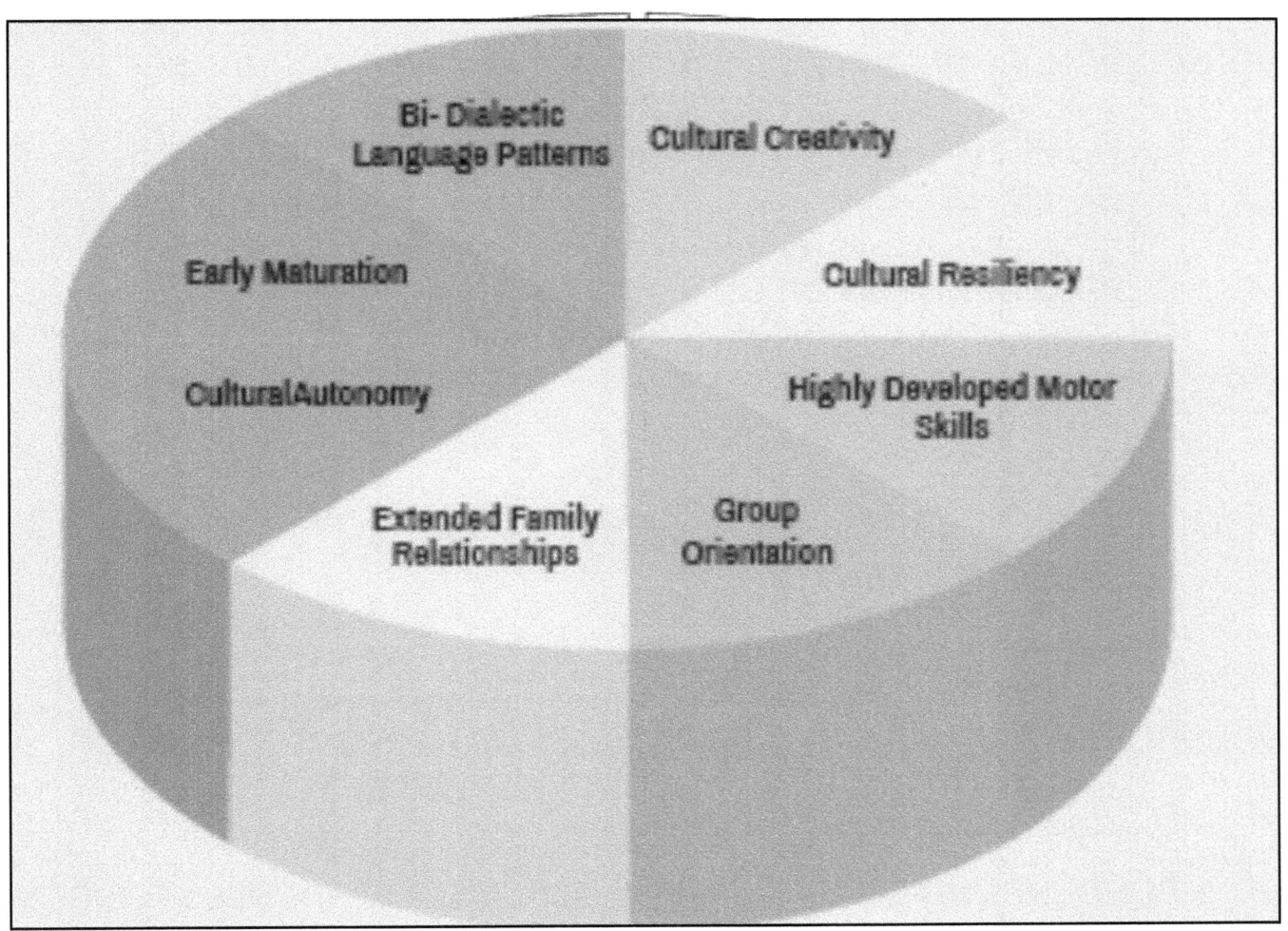

REVIEW QUESTIONS FOCUSING ON THE BLACK SOCIO-CULTURAL COGNITIVE LEARNING STYLE MATRIX

1. What is the Matrix development process of the Black Socio-Cultural Cognitive Learning Style?
2. Define each variable in the Matrix.
3. How does the life-style of African American children affect their socio-cultural learning style development?
4. How can teachers identify the characteristics identified in the Black Socio-Cultural Cognitive Learning Style?
5. Discuss each variable that makes up the Black Socio-Cultural Cognitive Learning Style to enhance teaching/learning in the classroom.
6. How can teachers best utilize information concerning the Black Socio-Cultural Cognitive Learning Style?
7. How can teachers effectively and sensitively teach African American students after identifying strengths and skills in the Black Socio-Cultural Cognitive Learning Style.
8. How does the Black Socio-Cultural Cognitive Learning Style differ from the learning style of white middle-class students?
9. How does the bilingual variable identified in the Black Socio-Cultural Cognitive Learning Style Model affect the learning ability of African American children in relation to standard English?
10. What are some possible affects on African American children if teachers and school officials do not understand the significance of culture as it relates to learning?

OTHER FACTORS, IMPLICATIONS & QUESTIONS RELATING TO THE BLACK SOCIO-CULTURAL COGNITIVE LEARNING STYLE

Research on the Black Socio-Cultural Cognitive Learning Style indicates that Black children are more academically capable than they are given credit for, just as the Black family structure and environment is not as socially bankrupted, as some researchers would like us to believe. The reality is that the majority of Black families are hard working, intact families, which includes both parents. All Black children do not use drugs, nor live in a drug infested environment. While it is true that a large percentage of Black children in the inner cities come from an impoverished home, being poor does not make a person intellectually inferior to others.

Poor academic performance is, instead, the results of a number of external and internal factors which has such a tremendous impact on the learning environment over which Black children have no control. For instance, Black children do not select their teachers. These children have no control of what type of individual they are made to interact with for six or more hours a day. Nor do these children design or select the curriculum or the environment of the classroom.

To this you might say "neither do white children." But that's not true. The philosophy, beliefs, curriculum and purpose of the public school system is presented in a European context. Therefore, white children have a built-in advantage and assurances when it comes to curriculum, beliefs and all other aspects of the school system. The school system is not just an "American" idea. It is a white American idea. White children benefit simply because they are white and these advantages have resulted in better academic performance for these students.

A good analogy of this historical arrangement in which Black students are at a clear disadvantage would be like forcing Israeli students to attend Arab schools, or South African White children to attend Black schools in South Africa. The harmful thing here is not the cultural shock which would occur for these students, but the fact that their academic performance would also be based on the cultural agenda established by school officials.

But culture isn't the only criteria used to create illusions. White society also uses wealth as a social determiner to treat impoverished people differently than those individuals from the white middle-class. It is this treatment which creates the illusion of inferiority. If the concept of American schools is to be schools for all Americans, then these schools would have to be multi-culture in nature in terms of testing, language, curriculum, personnel, beliefs, attitudes and philosophy representing a cultural fusion of all American cultures.

Instead, the schools are monolistic in nature and designed, primarily, to reflect the norms and values of white Americans. Until that changes, Black children will continue to encounter a number of external obstacles which must be resolved successfully in order for them to excel academically (See Diagram - Other Factors). Additional external obstacles include:

> * Teachers attitudes & perceptions
> * School curriculum & testing
> * School philosophy
> * Perpetuation of white-middle class values
> * Cultural/social racism
> * Cultural conflict
> * Teacher sensitivity
> * Motivation
> * Community Input
> * Family
> * Values & beliefs
> * School philosophy

****

OTHER FACTORS/IMPLICATIONS RELATING TO THE BLACK SOCIO-CULTURAL COGNITIVE LEARNING STYLE

Section III

The Process of Learning

The process of learning is very complex for a number of reasons: One, human beings are highly diverse intellectually, physically and culturally. Consequently, what they bring to any learning situation is diverse. Second, learning depends on, and thus involves, a number of intricate mental processes such as perceptions, emotions and feelings. All of which impact the entire learning process thereby influencing what is learned, how it is learned and even if it is learned at all.

There are many theories regarding learning ranging from the more popular Stimulus & Response Theory, to the more contemporary Contextual Theories which examine culture and environment as important aspects of learning. These theories vary greatly in how they define learning and what variables or components are essential in order for learning to occur. Indeed, theories on learning are as diverse as the very process they attempt to define.

Behaviorists, for example, view learning as a change in the behavioral disposition of an organism that is caused by experience and not explained on the basis of reflexes, maturation or temporary states. These theorists feel that learning occurs as a result of:

1. Direct exposure (i.e., conditioning reinforcement, etc)
2. Observation (i.e., role models, social learning, cultural learning etc.)
3. Language (i.e., verbal and written instruction, commands, directives, etc)

Cognitive Theorists, on the other hand, suggest that learning is the result of changes in the individual's knowledge of the world as a result of life-experiences. For these theorists, learning involves both Affective and Cognitive Components. The Process of Learning Model illustrates the interaction and interdependency of the Affective and Cognitive Components that are essential to the learning process:

AFFECTIVE COMPONENTS (Feeling & Thinking)

Motivation - desire, stimuli, reward, etc
Perception - values, beliefs, conditioning, culture

COGNITIVE COMPONENTS (Ability & Skills)

Rate/degree of learning - slow, fast, constant, etc
Transference - encoding, physical condition, etc
Retention - memory - short/long term etc

All of these variables are interrelated. That is, they all play equally important roles in the process of learning. All of the components must be present if learning is to take place. Obviously, numerous other variables impact the learning process. However, these are very essential components in the learning process. Unfortunately, since its inception the school system has traditionally manipulated the learning process to protect the status quo. Historically, very significant variables critical to learning were not considered important variables in the learning process and were ignored. Variables such as:

- Culture
- Environment
- Nutrition
- Student's perception
- Self-image and Self-esteem

Researchers today, however, now insist that these variables are critical to the learning process. More educators are talking to each other and there is more talk today about multi-cultural education, pluralism, balanced curriculum, teacher accountability, a national curriculum and the quality of education than ever before. Debating and examining these and similar subjects can only end in improving the nation's public school system. However, educators and teachers can only bring about relevant change and improvement to the public school system when they are willing to refocus their attention on understanding the Process of Learning.

****

THE PROCESS OF LEARNING

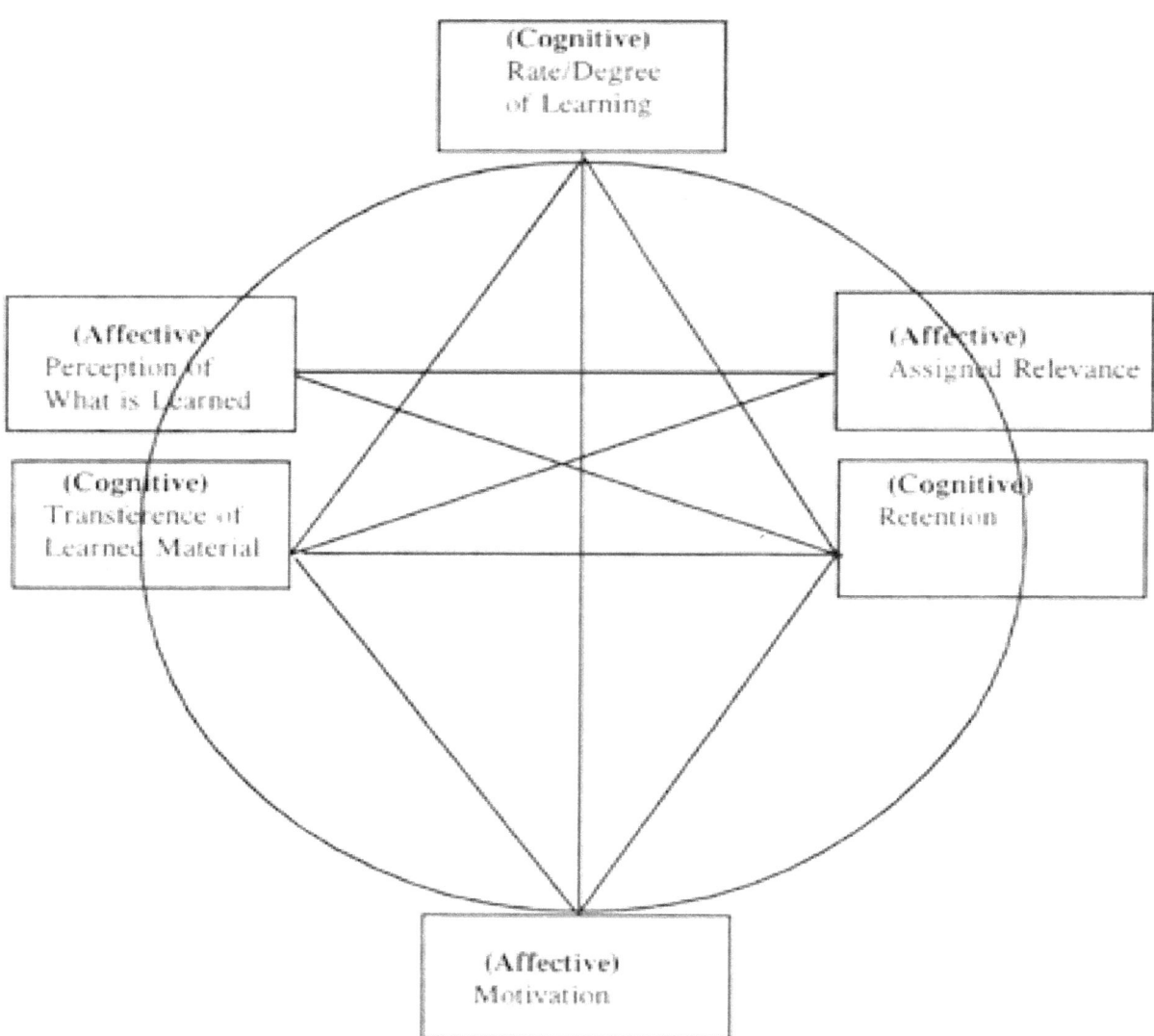

c1983Sessoms

Section IV

Cognitive Learning Styles

Cognition is defined as the way individuals learn to absorb information about their physical and social world. Researchers in the area of cognition seek to understand the process of learning, how information is retained and what social, cultural, psychological and physiological processes are involved in this process. Every aspect of human life involves cognition: how we think, how we perceive others, how we communicate, how we get long and even how we drive a car. As a mental process, cognition impacts our cultural and social values, language, creativity, imagery, perception, self-image, and self-esteem.

In education the study of cognition is important because it enables educators to come up with effective programs to facilitate learning. It also enables educators to develop beneficial intervention programs. Since the establishment of the public school system educators and teachers have wrestled with the task of educating the young of the society. During the early stages of development, educators were not overly concerned with high-sounding theories on learning and cognition. Instead, the focus was on teaching children basic skills.

Interest and research in cognition developed slowly during the early 1900's. From this array of research a number of major schools of thought emerged as a way of understanding learning and the cognitive process. Jean Piaget (1896-1980) well known for his extensive research on cognition, led the field in cognitive development. It was Piaget's work, first in biology and later in psychology, which documented for the first time new ways of looking at learning. Piaget believed that intelligence was a form of biological adaptation that allows the organism to survive and adapt to the environment. Central to his theory of cognition was the idea that learning occurs in stages and that for each individual the learning process is different.

Since that time other theories regarding cognition have been formulated. These include: Organismic Development Theories, Information Processing Theories, Behavioristic Theories, and more recently, Contextualistic Theories. All of these theories provide educators with additional information on the process of learning. More importantly, all of these theories suggest that individuals learn differently and all individuals possess a cognitive learning style that is highly diversified and uniquely different from others.

The National Task Force on Learning Styles and Brain Behavior adopted the following definition of learning styles.

COGNITIVE LEARNING STYLES

Learning Style is that consistent pattern of behavior and performance by which an individual approaches educational experiences. It is the composite of characteristic cognitive, affective and physiological behaviors that serve as relatively stable indicators of how a learner perceives, interacts with, and responds to the learning environment. It is formed in the deep structure of neural organization and personality which molds and is molded by human development and the cultural experiences of home, school and society.

From: James W. Keefe and Marlin Lanquis, "Learning Stages Network," Newsletter 4, No. 2 (Summer, 1983):1.

Section V ———————

Skills & Attributes of Black Students Identified by the Matrix Development of the Black Socio-Cultural Cognitive Learning Style

The Matrix Development Model identifies a number of skills, attributes, characteristics and abilities of Black children which develop as a result of the family, culture, environment, as defined by the Black Socio-Cultural Cognitive Learning Style. These include:

Extended Family Relationships -	Cultural Resiliency	Cultural Creativity	Early Maturation
Close kinship ties Interpersonal skills Numerous role models Strong family/group Identity Feeling of cooperation vs competition	Unique window of reality Race awareness at an early age Group identity/group ties Enhances self-image Value conflict Assimilation, acculturation	Ability to improvise Problem-solving ability Personable Very expressive Observational skills Ability to memorize complex data	Clearly defined, active Considered an essential member of family Defined responsibilities Flexible Cooperative and non-competitive
Group Orientation	**Environmental Autonomy**	**Expanded Language Pattern**	**Highly Developed Motor Skills**
Close group identity. Analytical skills. Ability to differentiate. Ability to make distinctions. Able to develop sound strategies for problem solving.	Able to make choices Flexible in interaction with others No rigid time structure Adapts well to most environments Screens sensory stimuli present Draws conclusions about others Responses creatively to personal environment	Bio-dialectic language pattern Uses language in a highly creative manner linguistically adaptable	Physical agility Ability to perform complex motor tasks Very creative and can improvise in play Analogical and propositional Conceptualizes movements easily

CHARACTERISTICS & PATTERN OF RESPONSE OF BLACK STUDENTS BASED ON THE BLACK SOCIO-CULTURAL COGNITIVE LEARNING STYLE MODEL

Research on the Black Socio-Cultural Cognitive Learning Style suggest that African American children are most likely to exhibit the following learning style characteristics and respond in very cultural-specific ways in certain situations as a result of their socio-cultural development:

CHARACTERISTICS:

* Highly Creative	* Concrete vs Abstract
* Independent learners	* Cooperative vs competitive
* Highly perceptive	* Observational learners
* Exhibits highly developed motor skills	* Bilingual

PATTERN OF RESPONSE

A. Classroom Interaction

√ Likes to communicated with other students in class.
√ Does not respond well in a rigid classroom setting.
√ Likes to work in small groups.
√ Likes to work as a team member.
√ Likes to work on fun type activities involving other classmates.

B. Curriculum Design

√ Tends to like curriculum that focuses on global activities.
√ Likes to work on activities that elicit feelings or opinions.
√ Reflects analytical skills in solving problems.
√ Tends to respond well to group activities.

√ Likes to work on activities that are practical and useful.

√ Prefers to work on activities that require imagination and intuition.

C. Communications with Teacher

√ Responds well to teachers who are sensitive and caring.

√ Responds well to positive feedback from teachers.

√ Tends to prefer immediate feedback from teacher when working on task.

√ Likes to receive personal recognition and attention from teacher.

√ Communicates well with teachers who appear to respect and appreciate their effort.

D. Instructional Design

√ Responds well to teachers who focus on content that elicits feelings and emotions.

√ Responds well to group activities.

√ Exhibit short attention span on various activities not related to culture, life style or what is perceived as relevant.

√ Responds to external cues when giving answers to problems and questions.

√ Learns best by relating personal experiences to instructional content.

√ Responds well to activities that are presented with various approaches (i.e., story telling).

****

RESEARCH RELATED TO THE BLACK SOCIO-CULTURAL COGNITIVE LEARNING STYLE

Perception is the basic process of cognition as it is the process through which the living organism maintains contact with the environment. (Travers, 1982) Thus, it is clear that perception is influenced by one's socialization and past experiences. Research is the premise upon which sound theories are based. Many experts in the field of Cognitive Development have not usually focused on cultural elements when developing these theories.

However, The Black Socio-Cultural Cognitive Learning Style (BSCCLS) is based on the efforts of very aware and competent researchers and educators who have conducted research over the years that address the critical areas of the cognitive learning styles of Black children, their specific cultural preferences and their intellectual strengths. Each specific variable which comprises the Black Socio-Cultural Cognitive Learning Style identifies in the Matrix Model has a sound premise that verifies each variable as a key factor in understanding how Black children learn.

Each variable is supported and corroborated by precise and credible research. Unfortunately, due to limited space, all relevant research studies and writings on the specific learning style of Black children can not be presented here. Following is a brief description of some of the research on the cognitive learning style of Black children. Obviously, there is still considerable research to be conducted in this area.

RESEARCH RELATED TO THE EIGHT DISTINCT VARIABLES IDENTIFIED IN THE MATRIX MODEL OF THE BLACK SOCIO-CULTURAL COGNITIVE LEARNING STYLE

SKILL IDENTIFIED: (Cognitive/Affective) EXTENDED FAMILY

Research Source: Asfhenbrenner (1972), Martain (1978) Description of Research Study: Black families are usually multi-generational, and expanded in nature with broad social networks of family, friends and relatives.

Research Source: Young (1970 & 1974) Description of Research Study: Black children are trained in the concept of collective responsibility.

Research Source: Sigel, Anderson & Shapiro (1966) Description of Research Study: Black children emphasize focusing on individuals rather than on non-person cues in the learning process Research Source: Brown (1982) Description of Research Study: Black children tend to categorize objects based on pictorial representation in holistic and relational manner

SKILL IDENTIFIED: (Cognitive/Affective) CULTURAL RESILIENCY

Research Source: White (1984) **Description of Research Study:** Black children do not believe that conformity to white values, involving language, time management, future orientation and competition will get them a viable job

SKILL IDENTIFIED: (Cognitive/Affective) CULTURAL CREATIVITY

Research Source: Farley (1981) **Description of Research Study:** Black children exhibiting high stimulation or exterversion is believed to be predictive of creative performance and a highly creative personality

Research Source: Richman (1971) **Description of Research Study:** Black children do better on tests on figural elaboration than white children. This task is seen as a test of the ability to elaborate, embellish, and develop ideas utilizing a high degree of sensitivity in observation

Research Source: Boykin (1979) **Description of Research Study:** Black children seem to prefer and need a variety of information at a constantly changing pace and have very little tolerance for monotonous or low-level activities as opposed to white children

SKILL IDENTIFIED: (Cognitive/Affective) EARLY MATURATION
Research Source: Baumrind (1972) **Description of Research Study:** Black female children are expected to be more mature. They demonstrate unusual social maturity and a wide range of adaptive behavior

SKILL IDENTIFIED: (Cognitive/Affective) GROUP ORIENTATION
Research Source: Gutes, Black & Montgomery (1972) **Description of Research Source:** Black children are people oriented people, exhibiting more feelings and emotions
Research Source: Guper (1973), Chance, Goldstein & McBride (1975) **Description of Research Study:** Black children utilize more social and people cues found in literature and place a great deal of emphasis on recognition of faces/emotions
Research Source: Demano (1983) **Description of Research Study:** Black children tend to include people such as teachers, classmates, etc., in their pictures while white children depict objects on physical settings

SKILL IDENTIFIED: (Cognitive/Affective) ENVIRONMENTAL AUTONOMY
Research Source: Cohen (1976), Hale (1982) **Description of Research Study:** The learning style of Black children tends to be rational and field dependent. This means that they tend to function better in cooperative information and loosely structured environments

SKILL IDENTIFIED: (Cognitive/Affective) BIO-DIALECTIC LANGUAGE PATTERNS
Research Source: Cohen (1969), Witkins (1971), Labov (1970) **Description of Research Study:** Black children tend to be holistic thinkers, select language from their social orientation through lack of distance, sue of transitional features and extensive use of concrete imagery

SKILL IDENTIFIED: (Cognitive) BIO-DIALECTIC LANGUAGE PATTERNS
Research Source: Cooper (1980), Houston (1970) **Description of Research Study:** Bio-dialectic language patterns of Black children who are holistic

thinkers, is based on the traditional Black culture which reinforces this type of thinking

SKILL IDENTIFIED: (Cognitive) HIGHLY DEVELOPED MOTOR SKILLS

Research Source: Pavenstedt & assoc. (1987) **Description of Research Study:** Black children were rather advanced in motor development and seem to use visual perception differently than white children

Research Source: Morgan (1981) **Description of Research Study:** Black children have a higher motor capability due to their apparent sensorimotor precocity

Research Source: Abstyne & Osburn (1937) **Description of Research Study:** Black children are as high as 50% better than white children in following rhythms

Research Source: Stringer (1940) **Description of Research Study:** Black children are superior in their ability to perceive the slightest body movement

****

TEACHING EFFECTIVELY TO THE BLACK SOCIO-CULTURAL COGNITIVE LEARNING STYLE

The majority of educators and teachers in the public school system have historically viewed the education of low-income, ethnic minority children as one of assimilation and acculturation into mainstream America. This approach carried with it silent messages which were ethnocentric and, thus, negative. However, to justify this view, and thereby, this approach in educating ethnic minorities, considerable research was conducted in an attempt to prove that ethnic minority children were academically inferior to white children. For decades researchers such as Ausbel (1965) and others, suggested that ethnic minority children, especially Black children were genetically and academically inferior to white children. Over the years these views have persisted. Research conducted by Jensen (1960) and other cultural deprivation theorists continue to perpetuate this inaccurate, misleading and racist concept regarding the educable ability of ethnic minority children.

From this research a host of ethnocentric and negative terms were used to describe non-white children. Some of the most commonly used terms include:

* Culturally deprived
* Environmentally deprived
* Aggressive
* Deviant behavior
* Disruptive
* Intellectually dysfunctional
* Culturally & socially disadvantaged
* Dysfunctional family structure
* Having irreversible cognitive deficient
* Poor language development (deficit hypothesis)

* Socially deprived
* Disadvantaged
* Slow learners
* Pre-academic deficiencies
* Lazy, trouble makers

The long term use of these negative terms and stereotypes resulted in the development of a host of misconceptions and unflattering images about non-white children. This also resulted in the development of an official unwritten policy, about non-white children. This policy defined nonwhite children, especially Black children, as being culturally and socially deprived, intellectually inferior, unmotivated and sometimes, even uneducable.

The perpetuation of these negative stereotypic images reflects the on-going cultural assault against non-white children so pervasive in the public school system. These images and negative terms conjure up false images and severely corrupt the classroom and the teaching environment. More importantly, these terms dramatically stifles the learning process of ethnic minority children.

Fortunately, as a result of the Civil Rights Movement of the 1960's, there has been a softening of these attitudes towards Black and other ethnic minorities. However, a residue of these same attitudes still exist. There still remains broad, sweeping discrepancies between the personal and cultural values and beliefs of teachers and ethnic minority students.

Research on the Black Socio-Cultural Cognitive Learning Style is an attempt to improve the educational experience for Black students and to assist teachers who teach them, part of this requires that we address existing attitudes, beliefs and conditions of both Black students and their teachers in a realistic manner. The Matrix Model of the Black Socio-Cultural Cognitive Learning Style identifies previously unacknowledged strengths of Black children. Based on this information we can begin the process of implementing this sweeping array of new information into the learning environment, thereby enhancing educational potentials of Black students.

What is needed now is the wisdom and vision to explore new possibilities and alternatives to the old way of educating non-white children and the courage to integrate this information into our teaching strategies. This section of the Handbook contains an assortment of models, teaching strategies and exercises that are designed to be informative and useful in the instruction of Black children based on the information identified in the Black Socio-Cultural Cognitive Learning Style.

****

TEACHING STYLE

"Teaching Style is a reflection of the individual's value system regarding human nature and the kinds of goals and environment that enhances human learning. One's teaching style represents a conscious of unconscious enacting of the way one prefers to learn and remember being taught."

Robert J. Hanson and Harvey Silvers, "Teaching Styles and Strategies," Hanson, Silver, Strong & Associates, Inc. Morristown. NJ.

Section VI ━━━━━━━━━━━━━━━━━━━━━

Teaching Skills Necessary to Effectively Teach Black Students

In recent decades the controversy surrounding teacher accountability and educational reform has intensified. Critics of the school system point to the alarming rate of high school dropouts, rising failure rates and plunging SAT scores. The recent publication of academic standing in math, science and history showed the United States behind South Korea, the new Russian state and China.

Central to the argument for school reform is the issue of widespread academic under achievement of a large percentage of Black students in our inner cities. In some urban areas dropout rates are as high as 50%. Poor academic achievement is by inner city Blacks is at its highest rate in years. One of the reasons cited for this troubling statistic is that there is a culture gap between the teachers who work in inner cities and the students they serve.

Research suggests that the majority of teachers working with inner city students are not adequately prepared to teach ethnically diverse students effectively. As educators, we can no longer afford to assume that all teachers who go through a teacher certification program leave these programs with the skills necessary to teach Black children effectively. Just as we can no longer assume that a degree or certificate in education prepares an individual to teach in a multi-culture environment. Most teacher education programs place little emphasis on multi-culture education or prepare these aspiring teachers to teach to diverse student populations.

Effective teaching requires that teachers possess a variety of skills and characteristics necessary to motivate, stimulate and communicate with students in the learning environment. These skills are essential if learning is to take place. This is especially true if these students happen to be ethnically different students.

The Black Socio-Cultural Cognitive Learning Style identifies a number of characteristics of African American children which teachers should be aware of in the teaching situation. These children are very observant, intuitive and are highly skilled at picking up silent messages from others. Today's teachers and administrators must demonstrate that they believe in the students ability to achieve or run the risk of failing to provide an adequate education for their ethnically diverse students.

The most essential skills required to teach ethnically diverse students include:

Communication Skills   Motivational Skills
Cross-Culture Communication Skills Holistic teaching skills
Problem solving skills   Strong diagnostic & assessment skills

CROSS CULTURAL COMMUNICATION

In recent years the public school system has witnessed a dramatic change in the racial composition of the student population served. Originally the public school system was designed to educate the young based on the values, beliefs and customs of the white middle class. Now the classrooms are predominantly black and a large percentage of those students now served are from low-income, ethnic minority groups. This has resulted in a dilemma for educators who must now deal cross-culturally with a group of students who don't share the same culture, values, beliefs, traditions or customs. In response to these rapidly changing demographics and what appears to be a crisis in the school system, educators are focusing more on multi-culture education in an attempt to address the issue of ethnicity.

It is hoped that by doing so some of the more serious problems will be solved: high rates of academic failure, low SAT scores, rising absenteeism and mounting drop-out rates, drugs, teenage pregnancy, and gangs. School districts across the nation have sought solutions to these problems in different ways. Some have opted to hiring more ethnic minority staff to provide students with effective role models; some districts have focused on expanding the curriculum to be more inclusive of ethnic minorities. Most, however, have focused on the issue of cross-culture communications in response to a school population which is becoming increasingly nonwhite.

Defined, cross-culture communication means active communication between individuals from different cultures. In education, cross-culture communication has come to mean communication between teachers and students from different ethnic backgrounds. More precisely, it means communications between teachers who are representative of the dominant white European culture and students who are outside of the mainstream in terms of culture, socio-economic status and life experiences.

All students enter the classroom with pre-defined cultural attributes, such as those described in the Matrix Model of the Black Socio-Cultural Cognitive Learning Style. The Model illustrates how variables such as family, culture and environment influence how Black children will respond in the classroom. It also demonstrates how Black students will communicate with others based on this culture-specific mode of communications.

Communication experts are quick to point out that there is a vast difference between communications used in a homogenous setting and communication between people from different cultures. Consequently, in addition to be cognizant to the rules of communication, teachers must also be aware of the importance of culture in the communication process.

Teachers seeking to develop strong cross-culture communication skills must be culturally and socially aware of the impact of ethnicity on the process of communications. In addition, since teachers are in control of the classroom situation, they must lay the ground work for effective, empowering cross-culture communications.

Effective cross-cultural communication requires hard work and a sincere commitment on the part of teachers. It also involves patience and enthusiasm. Keep in mind that developing excellent cross-cultural communication skills is a highly complex process which involves mutual acceptance and respect.

****

PROBLEM SOLVING SKILLS

Strong, fundamental problem-solving skills are essential in the learning process. Teachers must be able to recognize a problem in the classroom environment, whether it involves academic ability, teaching style or personal classroom interaction. However, the problem-solving process itself becomes more complex when culture is introduced as a variable because it impacts a number of areas crucial to the learning situation: the tone of the classroom environment, students responses, self-esteem and student/teacher relationships.

The ability to properly assess a situation and make accurate decisions based on this assessment is critical to teaching. How well a teacher is able to problem-solve greatly impacts learning. Teachers are expected to devise techniques and strategies to facilitate learning to help students learn to solve problems regarding course work. Students are taught critical thinking strategies which will aid and direct them in finding solutions to classroom problems. Problem-solving in the classroom can be classified as either academic or culture-specific processes. In terms of academic problem-solving skills, teachers are expected to teach students how to master certain classroom materials to meet the school's academic requirements. This type of problem solving follows a logical procedure and is central to the teaching process.

Research shows that problem-solving involves a number of techniques and strategies which can be learned and improved upon. Ralph L. Pounds and James R. Bryner (1973) in their book, "The School in American Society" identified the steps involved in the problem solving process:

1. An awareness of the problem.
2. Clarification of the problem.
3. Definition of needed data - construction of a "search model."
4. Collection and organization of data.
5. Formulation of tentative hypotheses.
6. Logical testing of hypotheses.
7. Drawing of conclusions.
8. Testing of conclusions:
    -   logically
    -   empirically

These technique can be introduced to students lacking strong problem-solving skills and these skills can be useful in solving problems in everyday situations.

The second type of problem-solving skill teachers should master involves culture-specific problems that impact the learning situation. These problems can occur as a result of a classroom crisis or as a personal or behavioral problem involving one or several students. These types of problems emerge in all classrooms. Being a creative problem-solver is a valuable asset for teachers who, in a multi-culture classroom, are constantly called upon to solve culture-specific problems. Cultural awareness, sensitivity and a sincere commitment on the part of the teacher to resolve these problems in an equable manner is essential if teachers are to be successful in teaching ethnic minority students.

Research on the Black Socio-Cultural Cognitive Learning Style suggests that Black students respond more favorably to a teacher who appears to be fair, sensitive and caring in response to problem solving in the classroom. In a multi-culture classroom most problems are usually the result of cultural diversity. Minimizing cultural differences results in confusion for both the student and the teacher.

Research shows that acquiring effective problem solving skills for use in a multi-culture situation requires that teachers have a strong knowledge of the history of various cultural groups and the ability to understand how traits and characteristics are related to skills. Teachers must know, for example, how to develop and build relationships with students that are positive and empowering. Developing strong problem solving skills happens as a result of personal experience and educational training. However, developing adequate problem-solving skills that are needed in solving social, cultural and psychological problems requires that teachers:

1. Have a clear understanding of the cultural aspects of the problem.
2. Define what is needed to solve the problem.
3. Have a prior knowledge of the problem or similar problems.
4. Have problem solving experience.
5. Have the ability to be empathetic.
6. Be able to demonstrate sensitivity.
7. Be creative in the problem solving process.
8. Be empowering.
9. Offer encouragement.
10. Acknowledge efforts.
11. Develop reasonable reward system.
12. Able to admit that you might be wrong.

As educators we must remember that it is not always important to be in total control or to insist on correct answers. Sometimes the "end" does not justify the "means". Problem-solving requires the ability to be flexible; sometimes the seemingly correct solution is not necessarily the most appropriate answer for the situation. When problem-solving in the classroom consideration must be given cultural, social and the personal characteristics of the student. In essence, strong problem solving skills will greatly enhance the learning environment by keeping teachers cognizant of students as individuals with very unique qualities and culture-specific personalities.

DIAGNOSTIC SKILLS

Testing, evaluating and diagnosing the academic ability of students in an important job of the public school system. Presently the school system utilized several types of tests to determine grade level and placement of student. These tests include: Wechsler Intelligence Scale for Children (WISC), SAT, Stanford-Binet, Iowa Basic Skills Battery, Gates Reading Test and a host of other multi-test aptitude batteries.

Considerable research has been devoted to the value of such testing. There is a prevailing consensus among many researchers that most of these tests are Eurocentric in nature and are aimed at, thereby benefiting, white middle class students. In addition to being perceived by many as being racially bias, there are a number of other objections to the practice of diagnostic testing used by the public schools. These objections include:

1. These tests are detrimental to nonwhite children and has resulted in the mis-education of these children.
2. These tests are too limited in nature to truly assess the educational potential of nonwhite children.
3. The evaluation process used by the public school system is highly subjective and runs the risk of discriminating against those students who do not meet the criteria of teachers in terms of personality, culture, lifestyle and behavior.
4. Too much emphasis is placed on these tests in the process of determining academic ability and grade level.

Furthermore, the impact of such testing has far reaching implications primarily because these tests can (and do) determine the educational experience of students. By placing so much emphasis on these tests we are ignoring the more critical components of learning. We ignore, for example, the impact of culture, life experiences, values and self-esteem. However, in spite of this and the controversy surrounding the use of such tests, we still use them. As a result, across the nation a disproportionate number of Blacks and other ethnic minority students are placed in low-track. Special Education Classes. These placements are based, primarily on these inappropriate tests and misguided recommendations from teachers.

Academic testing and achievement grouping, however, is not the only area of concern. How teachers arrive at these assessments and react to the behavior of non-white students is also a critical issue in the public school system. Research on the Black Socio-Cultural Cognitive Learning Style demonstrates that teachers often misinterpret the behavior of non-white students primarily because of existing differences in culture, values, beliefs and lifestyles. In the school system the teacher is a representative or articulates the belief system of the white middle class. Thus, the behavior of non white students, whose culture is different, is often misunderstood from a cultural and social perspective.

Research studies on school discipline shows that Black students are more likely to be expelled, suspended or severely disciplined in greater numbers than white students committing the same offenses. This happens as a result of lack of cultural awareness on the part of he teachers and very subjective, culturally based judgment calls. Teachers who are unskilled in working with ethnically diverse students are themselves products of poor teacher education programs and a public school system which is, by nature, a middle class institution. These teachers bring with them into the classroom a host of unfounded, misleading perceptions and stereotypes about their ethnically different students.

For the majority of teachers teaching in public schools an assignment to an inner city, urban ghetto school is highly undesirable. Most teachers enter these schools with a middle-class orientation of the students being served. This dramatically impedes the educational development of non-white children, primarily because of the broad differences in orientation. Black students, and other ethnically diverse students, are likely to be perceived as difficult to teach, aggressive, loud, lazy, talkative, rebellious, troublemakers, unmotivated, uncontrollable, slow learners and disruptive.

Conceptually, these negative perceptions impact both the teaching and learning process. Those teachers who, consciously or unconsciously, perceive ethnic minority students in this way are denying these students real educational opportunities. Teachers must be able to properly assess and understand culture-specific behavior of their non-white students. This is a direly needed skill for those teachers teaching in urban area schools. Moreover, strong diagnostic skills are a prerequisite to being an excellent teacher. As educators we must begin to realize that for non-white students the wrong academic diagnostic or a gross misinterpretation of a student's behavior can have a long-lasting impact on the total academic life of that student. We must work hard to develop the skills we need to properly assess and evaluate those students we serve.

****

MOTIVATIONAL SKILLS

There are a number of theories regarding motivation. Some researchers regard motivation as a function of a person's thoughts, nothing more. On the other hand, Maslow and other humanists view motivation as an innate aspect of an individual's psyche. Regardless of your position on the subject of motivation, as educators we know that motivation is one of the most important "Teacher Skills" needed to teach ethnic minority students and is a prime factor in whether or not these students learn.

To motivate means to furnish a motive or motives; to give impetus to; incite; to impel. A motive is a moving cause; some inner drive, impulse, intention that causes a person to do something or act in a certain way; an incentive or goal. Research shows that all children entering school demonstrates a "natural excitement" toward learning. That is, all children are naturally motivated to learn in the early grades. However, this same research shows that as these children move through the school system this natural excitement diminishes or disappears altogether. As a result of this dilemma, teachers and educators are left with a school full of unmotivated, underachieving students.

Educators blame parents and poor parenting skills. Parents blame insensitive teaches with low expectations of minority students, uncommitted administrators and bureaucratic government agencies which seem to exist only to aggravate the problems. Community groups blame racism, lack of sensitivity on the part of teachers and public school officials, inadequate funding and lack of resources.

Obviously all of these factors have a tremendous impact on motivation and have been around for decades. However, we still haven't come up with the viable solutions needed to solve these problems and given the social climate of the 1990's there is no indication that we are closer now to solutions than we were twenty years ago. But learning how to motivate students does not take intense national involvement or millions of federal dollars in aid. What it does take is commitment and dedication to the proposition of education the young of the society on the part of teachers, administrators, community groups and parents.

We know, for example, that students who have a strong positive self-image, are more likely to be motivated than those with a negative self-image. Research on the Black Socio-Cultural Cognitive Learning Style demonstrates that Black children are very observant and highly sensitive to others in their environment. They are able to understand through visual cues of body language and voice tone, how others feel about them. How you, as a teacher, make your ethnic minority students feel in your classroom is paramount to motivation.

As educators, we have the advantage. We have been trained to motivate, to teach and to direct. It is not necessary to recreate the wheel - we are trained professionals. What we must do now is to rechannel our energies into the areas of motivation which is key to academic success of our students. More importantly, we must realize that motivation is a manifestation of commitment and sincere concern. Nothing less will work.

Following is the beginning of a list of factors which will cultivate motivational levels of students. You can personalize this list by adding, throughout the school year, new factors which work best for you and your students. To begin, you should make sure that.....

1. Students feel respected and cared for in your classroom.
2. There is no evidence of racism or cultural distinctions being made (by you or other students) in the classroom.
3. The classroom environment is nonthreatening, positive and multicultural.

HOLISTIC TEACHING SKILLS

 Holistic teaching is not a new concept in the field of education. It has been around for years. According to Hanoch Livneh and Ardis Sherwood (1991), holistic principles asserts that body, mind and soul, sensations thoughts, emotions and perceptions are all elements of the total organism. In order for teachers to teach ethnic minority students effectively they must, therefore, examine how they approach teaching and be prepared and willing to understand the total individual.

Teaching holistically requires that educators and teachers view students holistically. That is, to teach student by incorporation all aspects of the student's life and personality (i.e. family culture, learning style, preferences, community, etc) in the teaching process. Thus, the teaching environment is expanded to address and integrate all of these components in the learning situation. Obviously, teachers in the public school system are at a disadvantage here because of the ratio of the student/teacher relationship. But this does not mean that this approach to teaching should be ignored.

To teach from a holistic perspective does not require any outlandish preparations. What is does require is that teacher's approach the teaching situation with the understanding that students are, in fact, human beings with an already established set of values, beliefs and opinions which reflect who they are and which are credible and relevant. Thus, holistic teaching requires that teachers enter the teaching arena with the intent of providing students with a culture-free, non-racist atmosphere in which honestly, equality and openness prevails.

Holistic teaching is a humanistic approach to teaching because it diminishes the focus of control and discipline of learning from the official public school policy to what is important and relevant to the student in regards to fulfilling the student's academic potential. Holistic teaching requires that teaching professionals focus on the growth and self realization of the student, rather than on control and social adjustment.

Personal responsibility, rather than rigid discipline are essential to the teaching process and become, therefore, important by words when teaching holistically. Students are taught self responsibility in the learning situation. This concept of self responsibility empowers students by acknowledging existing individual social and cultural differences. It is not enough for teachers and educators to tell ethnic minorities that cultural and social differences are acceptable. They must be willing to continually demonstrate that these differences enrich and enhance the learning environment.

Black History Month, for example, would be discontinued and African-American curriculum and information fully integrated into mainstream curriculum. Cultural diversity would become an intricate component of the total make up of the public school system. Thus, African-American history would become an acceptable, normal aspect of learning, rather than information relegated to one period during the year. White students and other ethnic minority students would be required to learn this information as part of the general curriculum.

In addition, school officials would embrace cultural and ethnic diversity as an important ingredient in the teaching of young people. This would be reflected in the philosophy of the school, the hiring of staff and the relationships maintained with the surrounding community. Holistic education requires that teachers, administrators, parents, community groups and students learn to celebrate cultural and social differences and be willing to capitalize on the rich cultures in American society by learning from each other.

****

IMPLEMENTING COMMUNICATION SKILLS

Good communication is essential to teach effectively and for students to learn. Following are some ideas and suggestions for cultivating good communication skills in the classroom:

1. Encourage (or assign) your students to design a Communication Module for your classroom. Include information on all types of communication.
2. Make communications a part of your lesson plan. Allow students to identify various types of communications.
3. Use an award system when students demonstrate positive communications (smiling, voice tone, etc.).
4. When making assignments, have the students repeat verbal instructions.
5. Utilize visuals to demonstrate examples of good communication.
6. Provide students with both verbal and written instructions when possible.
7. Make time for those students who seem to be having problems following directions or understanding the assignment.
8. Encourage your students to ask questions.
9. Encourage your students to assist other students having problems understanding.
10. Don't ridicule of allow other students to make fun of those students who are having problems understanding assignments or doing classroom work.

IMPLEMENTING CROSS-CULTURE COMMUNICATION SKILLS

In addition to being creative and well trained, teachers working in urban area schools with ethnic minority students must have strong cross cultural communication skills. Following are some suggestions for improving your cross-cultural communication skills.

1. Recognize different ethnic modes of communication and language variations.
2. Cultivate a positive cross-culture communication process in the classroom.
3. Identify the communication strengths of students from various cultural backgrounds and build on these strengths.
4. Approach the issue of ethnicity objectively.
5. Preserve the linguistic integrity and cultural uniqueness of each students.
6. Reject language related stereotypes associated with different ethnic groups.
7. Stop making cultural assumptions!

FOR EXAMPLE:

1. Being silent does not necessarily mean that a child is not motivated or uncooperative. Silence means different things in different cultures. Teachers should attempt to be open to types of social interaction and not demand that students conform to the European model of communication.
2. It is not necessary to give up (or downplay) your cultural identity just to be accepted by African American students. Some White teachers try using street talk or slang when communications to African American students. Most African American students find this type of behavior funny; others consider it demeaning. Most will consider this type of behavior "stupid". It is not necessary to be "down" or "with it" to communicate effectively to African American students. It is necessary to be open and honest.

IMPLEMENTING PROBLEM-SOLVING SKILLS

To help student develop academic and culture specific problem solving skills teachers should consider the following:

1. Request a problem statement from each of your students.
2. Help your students define the problem.
3. Explain the problem solving process.
4. Identity alternative solutions with your students.
5. Summarize the alternatives identified.
6. Turn the list over to the student.
7. Let the student analyze the possible consequences of each alternative.
8. Have the student rate each alternative.
9. Let the student determine the best alternative.
10. Determine the student's satisfaction with choice selected.
11. State your support for the student's decision.
12. Ask the student if help is needed to take action.
13. Provide help in taking action if necessary. Ask those students who don't need any help to help another student.
14. Try to identify with the student additional alternatives.
15. Help the student select the best alternative.
16. Ask if help is needed to take action.
17. Provide help in taking action if necessary.

IMPLEMENTING HOLISTIC TEACHING SKILLS

Teaching holistically requires that teachers embrace the student as an important, significant individual with a unique set of life circumstances. Too often teachers depersonalize students in order to maintain control. Try the following:

1. Develop the ability to give positive feedback to students. This can be done by using phrases, illustrations and behavior that denotes positive feedback.

2. Develop the ability to articulate concepts to students in a nonthreatening manner.

3. Develop group dynamic skills to facilitate the learning process. Try to allow your students to elicit responses, engage in group projects and discussions, etc.

4. Approach the student by personalizing classroom interaction. Use first names and nicknames. This will give the student a sense of worth and identity.

5. Assign students classroom responsibilities in an equitable manner. This establishes trust and respect and also encourage students to become more involved in the total structure of the classroom. This will also encourage learning and develops motivation in the classroom environment.

6. Focus on motivation techniques. Do this by emphasizing culture as a relevant and important part of the curriculum. Encourage students to give suggestions on developing lesson plans and selecting curriculum.

7. Be consistent in dealing with your students. This creates a feeling of classroom unity and a feeling of equity and worth among students.

IMPLEMENTING MOTIVATIONAL SKILLS

1. Test anxiety - Help your students learn to cope with testing by providing a relaxing, test taking environment. Try new approaches with testing: get parents to give their children pre-type tests for practice; inform parents when a test is coming up; have a pretest party in the classroom.

2. Examining classroom procedures to make sure they are equitable and fair. Solicit suggestions from your students on how improvements can be made.

3. Be encouraging to students, especially during testing. Use positive phrases:
   - Do your best
   - Don't worry if your can't do some of the problems
   - The most important thing is that you try hard and do as well as you can
   - I know you will do a good job, even if you don't get all the questions right because
   - I know you are doing the very best job that you can

4. Make use of visual aid that denotes persistence, patience and determination. Make use of cartoons or familiar community figures/personalities.

5. Encourage students to make up a list of words that can be used daily in the classroom to encourage students to try hard and do their best.

6. Don't make assumptions about a student' ability.

7. Use verbal expressions regarding high expectations when dialoguing with students. Research shows that children who are treated as though they can not learn will eventually display this lack of ability (self-fulfilling prophecy).

8. Learn to reshape behavior. Reinforce positive academic achievement even if the student's performance was only marginal. A great many ethnic minority students have been told by so many people that they are "slow" or "an underachiever" that they begin to act out this type of behavior. To receive "praise" from the teacher, even though the student did not do exceptionally well on a test will encourage the student to continue to try.

9. Research shows that failure is a learned concept. That is, children at an early age are very confident that even though they failed at a task,

they can get it right with more effort. **De-emphasize failure and focus on success**. Congratulate your students on their accomplishments - regardless of how small the task might appear.

10. Provide your students with large doses of positive feedback, as individuals and as groups. This will help to raise their expectations of themselves, as individuals and as members of a group. The result of this will be an increase in a collective academic success oriented classroom and increase motivational levels.

11. Create high expectations for your students, learn to build confidence. Use positive phrases.

12. Be realistic when handing out classroom assignments - give your students some achievable goals/ classroom assignments.

13. Learn to channel preexisting motivation in a new direction. Have you ever wondered why a lot of students can recite, verbatim TV commercials, or sing a song after only hearing if once or twice? What motivates them?

14. Promote learning through instruction:
     ◦ Ask your students questions.
     ◦ Have students ask each other questions.
     ◦ Let students discover answers on their on through carefully planning learning maps using "hints."
     ◦ Let students do it themselves! Use as much "hand-on" classroom exercises as possible.
     ◦ Encourage students to work on their own or in small groups and to use each other as resources.
     ◦ Make use of:
          · peer learning
          · peer tutoring
          · chalk boards
          · audiovisual equipment
          · the concept of teamwork
          · experimental study programs
          · community resources (guest speakers, special professions, etc)
          · comic books, newspapers, television

Note: Please keep in mind that all these suggestions will work with any grade level and older students with very little modification

HOW TO TEACH EFFECTIVELY TO THE BLACK SOCIO-CULTURAL COGNITIVE LEARNING STYLE

1. Take the teacher's Cognitive Awareness/Assessment Instrument.

   ▪ Analyze your responses to the assessment tool.

2. Take the Cognitive Assessment Student Observational Instrument.

   ▪ Analyze your responses to that assessment tool.

3. Develop a curriculum plan.
4. Identify techniques and strategies to implement your curriculum plan.
5. Implement your curriculum plan.
6. Review the results of your curriculum plan.
7. Evaluate the positive and negative aspects of your curriculum.

After you have become familiar with the content assessment instrument, it is not necessary to follow step 1 and 2. Step 3-8 is necessary to follow if teachers are going to be effective teaching Black students. Taking the assessment instrument periodically is recommended in order to gain an introspective view of Black students.

Keep in mind that the scoring process is very subjective but it is designed to train teachers to work effectively with Black students. Usefulness of the instruments depends on an objective approach to the use of these instruments and clarity of purpose in answering each item. It is hoped that this exercise will provide teachers with a comprehensive view of their cultural awareness and sensitivity which should aid them in working effectively with African American students.

****

TEACHING STRATEGIES FOR WORKING WITH AFRICAN AMERICAN STUDENTS

Strategies refer to a variety of activities, techniques or methods that are devised to enhance the teaching/learning experience. In order to effectively teach Black children teachers must acquire information based on the cultural experiences of Black students to help increase the quality of teaching. Effective teaching utilizing information contained in the Black Socio-Cultural Cognitive Learning Style Matrix Model focuses on the following:

STRATEGIES FOR WORKING WITH BLACK STUDENTS

Creativity	The ability to be original and deviate from the norm in presenting concepts. *Black students usually find creative activities challenging.
Motivation	The ability to make learning relevant and challenging to Black students. *Black students respond well to highly enthusiastic teachers.
Self-questioning	Refers to reviewing one's own ability to impart knowledge or compare concepts. *Black children are very sensitive and can sense teachers who are knowledgeable and self-assured.
Effective Teaching	Refers to the ability to impart knowledge in a way that students are able to internalize concepts. *Black students are able to internalize knowledge that is presented in a diverse manner.
Learning Condition	Refers to creating an atmosphere that is conducive for learning. *Black students respond favorably when a caring and concerned environment is created.
Learning Activities	Refers to the development of techniques and methods of events or tasks which can enhance learning. *Black students interact positively with learning concepts that are meaningful.
Investigative Instruction	Refers to the ability to experiment and take risks. Being able to explore new techniques and methods in order become more effective. *Black students respond well to flexible modes of instructional styles.
Multi-Cultural Curricula	Refers to instructional activities that are culturally diverse. *Black students respond well to curriculum materials which focus on self-history or role models.

GENERAL PRINCIPLES to enhance the learning experience of African American students.

1. Build a positive climate in the classroom.
2. Develop a positive sense of group spirit/team work in the classroom.
3. Build on the strengths of your students.
4. Use humor as a method of control to increase student involvement and to develop group cohesiveness.
5. Give your students choices in problem-solving situations.
6. Use frequent and immediate "positive" feedback with your students.
7. Be noncritical, non-judgmental and accepting of all of your students. Research shows that teachers respond more favorably to those students for whom they have high expectations and negatively towards those students for whom they have low expectations.
8. Use open-ended questions when dialoguing with your students:
   * How do you feel about it?
   * What is it like?
   * Why do you feel that way?
   * What are your feelings about...?
   * What have you tried so far?

WORKING WITH AFRICAN AMERICAN STUDENTS: CLASSROOM MANAGEMENT

1. Use empathic, supportive statements with students who appear to be frustrated, angry or upset. Try to understand their point of view.

2. Use good supporting statements:
   * That's a good point!
   * You've got a good idea there.
   * You may be right.
   * Many people feel that way.

3. Acknowledge the student's opinion, even if you don't agree.

4. Use positive intonation in your voice and positive body language when interacting and talking with your students.

5. Allow sufficient wait-time when asking your students questions or during dialogue.

6. Try to incorporate ideas from students when formulating questions or during dialogue.

7. Build self-esteem through the use of encouragement and openness. Suggestions on how this might be accomplished:
   * Honoring students in front of the class.
   * Sharing some secret with the class and/or certain students.
   * Granting special favors as much as possible to students.
   * Try to be genuine in your concern for personal problems a student might be experiencing.
   * Try to respond to the uniqueness of each student and remember the long-term impact you can have on this student's life.
   * Encourage class discussions based on experiences of your students.

REMEMBER!!

Effective strategies must be based on making the learning experience relevant to the lives of your students if they are to learn meaningful concepts. When children are not actively responding to the curriculum, it may be necessary of resort to alternative strategies. Strategies and techniques can be critical to ultimately designing the most empowering and workable instructional plan, especially when working with African American students.

SUGGESTIONS FOR DEVELOPING
TEACHING STRATEGIES

1. Understand and appreciate cultural diversity.
2. Communicate openly, honestly and in a positive manner.
3. Develop activities to focus on the cognitive learning style of your students.
4. Group work.
5. Problem solving.
6. Use team projects whenever possible.
7. Modeling of concepts (practice what you preach...
8. Encourage cooperation and group interaction.
9. Don't be so concerned with "control"...democratize your classroom.
10. Discard old myths that some children just can't learn (self-fulfilling prophecy).
11. Be flexible and responsive to the needs of your students.
12. Don't make assumptions; don't be judgmental in your approach to your students.
13. Learn to appreciate yourself and your efforts.
14. Accept and acknowledge your unique abilities and your strengths. This positive attitudes will reflect favorably on your students.
15. Be good to yourself and your students.
16. Provide your students with every opportunity to master curriculum concepts and to feel respected for their efforts.
17. Strive to understand your students as other human beings first, and students second.
18. Encourage class discussions based on life experiences of your students.

TEACHING STRATEGIES TO INCORPORATE
ALL COGNITIVE LEARNING STYLES

1. Examine the curriculum being used in the classroom.
2. Examine the grading process used.
3. Is the teaching style used in the classroom monolistic?
4. Attempt to incorporate aspects of other culture throughout the classroom and teaching plans.
5. Expand on the use of role models in the classroom environment. Use people from various ethnic groups and from different professions.
6. Cultivate interaction respect among students.
7. Encourage interaction in the classroom.
8. Attempt to incorporate various instructional techniques for students who do not appear to be motivated.
9. Examine the classroom environment. Is it diverse? Is it functional?
10. Observe your students. Are they physically comfortable? Ill, hungry, or tired? Interested in something other than what is being offered.
11. Do you understand the needs of your students.
12. Are you teaching or pushing instead of helping? Talking, instead of demonstrating? Listening instead of ignoring?

TEACHING STRATEGIES IN
SPECIFIC CONTENT AREAS

SOCIAL STUDIES:

* Use newspapers, television or radio programs to teach social concepts related to African American community/culture.
* Use pictures of positive African American role models to build positive self-esteem.
* Use classroom discussions to encourage dialogue about real life situations to build social awareness.
* Plan lessons which emphasize the contributions of Black in the area of law, politics, art and music.
* Present famous African American Social Scientists as role models to enhance the self esteem of students.
* Create a nonthreatening, open classroom.
* Develop lesson plans using television programs based on cultural diversity.
* Develop lessons plans to incorporate African American students social skills.
* Develop lesson plans focusing on real current affairs to build social awareness.
* Develop lesson plans focusing of debates with students developing solutions for resolving various social issues.
* Focus on relevant issues such as having Black students conduct research on African Americans.
* When possible, let students identify areas of interest for assignments regarding contributions of African Americans.

MATH:

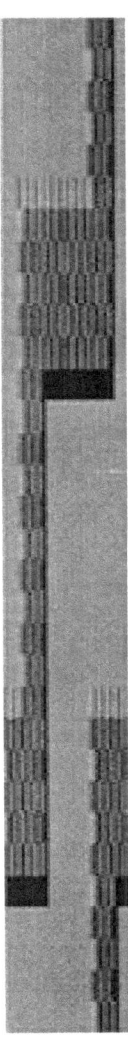

* Develop lesson plans utilizing video tapes/audio tapes which will allow students an opportunity to hear and/or see actual methods for solving certain types of math problems.
* Focus on the importance of math by utilizing explicit and practical examples from everyday life (food, candy, etc.).
* Present profiles of famous African American mathematicians as role models to enhance self-esteem of students.
* Focus on the student's prior knowledge of facts, rules and definitions to illustrate the relationship of math concepts.
* Assign students math projects according to their interest.
* Attempt to relate math problems with practical experiences in the homes of your students.
* Whenever possible use visual aids to illustrate mathematical concepts.
* Focus on areas of interest and difficulty in teaching practical mathematical concepts.
* Focus on discussion of everyday problems of mathematics (transactions involving money, etc).
* Plans lesson which will aid students in identifying practical objects that are used in computing everyday math skills.
* Develop math games to add variety to acquisition of math concepts.

ENGLISH/LANGUAGE ARTS

Research on the Black Socio-Cultural Cognitive Learning Style demonstrates that Black students enter school with a Bio-dialectic language pattern. That is, they use both standard English and Black English to define and describe their own life experiences and perceptions. This dual language pattern is a strength rather than a deficit. Teachers can greatly enhance the learning environment if they employ some of the following strategies when teaching Black students English and Language Arts.

* Don't correct a student for using Black English, especially in front of their peers. This can prove to be embarrassing to the students and can cause stress and anxiety.

* Build on English skills that the child already has. Have students write exactly what they feel, then go over corrections with students individually.
* Grade essays and writings on content rather than grammatical correctness.
* Use innovative ways in handling corrections to be made. For example, rewrite papers correctly and have the student copy it. This will say to the students that yes, I understand what you wrote, but this is another way it can be written.
* Explain why various aspects of English are necessary. Interject games into the teaching process, especially in teaching English.
* Assign students a certain part of the English language for a short period of time and require that they act out that part of English during discussions in English until they have internalized that particular rule of English.
* Stress vocabulary building, include words and expressions familiar to African American students. Build linkages between what is considered to be Black English and Standard English.
* Practice testing using the actual test. This way African American students can familiarize themselves with the type of questions that will be asked and learn to anticipate the type of responses required.

Utilizing some of the above suggestions will assist African American students in learning to view English as a positive aspect of learning, rather than as another way to devalue their language. These students will also learn to be more efficient at testing and will learn to enjoy English and Literature.

SCIENCE

* Relate science process skills with practical experiences in the homes of your students.
* Focus on the importance of science by utilizing explicit and practical example.
* Present profiles of famous Black scientists as role models to enhance the self-esteem of your students.
* Focus on the student's prior knowledge of facts, rules and definitions to illustrate the relationship of science concepts.

* Assign student's science projects according to their interest.
* Develop lesson plans to illustrate how science concepts relate to everyday life situations.
* Utilize field trips to give your students practical experiences.
* Use video tape presentations of basic, practical concepts of science with your students.
* Develop "fun type" science games to stimulate student involvement and interest in science.
* Develop lesson plans that focus on hands-on experiences, such as allowing your students to create their own inventions based on science concepts.
* Develop lesson plans which will encourage students to recognize the involvement of science in their everyday life.
* Be creative. Develop lesson plans designed to encourage Black students to create their own fantasies involving science concepts and skills.

MULTICULTURAL CURRICULUM

THE IMPORTANCE OF MULTI-CULTURE CURRICULUM

The type of curriculum used in the classroom is very critical to the teaching process and is certainly as equally important as the attitude of the teacher, and the classroom environment. Curriculum is fundamental to the learning process because it sets the stage for teaching by determining what is learned, how it is learned and why it is to be learned. Effective curriculum should be accurate, credible and interesting. This means that the curriculum content has to be diverse enough to include information of concern to all ethnic groups served by the nation's public schools.

Since the Civil Rights Movement of the 1960's, attempts have been made by many school officials to provide students with multi-culture curriculum which includes information on ethnic minorities. In recent years Black studies, Hispanic Studies, Asian Studies and Native American Studies have been added to most school programs, including colleges and universities. In addition, most school systems have set aside different periods of the year to focus exclusively on one ethnic group or another.

However, in spite of these energetic efforts on the part of most school officials to provide a culturally enriched curriculum, the problem has not gone away. The main reason is that there has never really been a serious commitment on the part of these school officials to truly integrate ethnic materials into the mainstream curriculum. Moreover, educators have been slow in demanding textbooks and curriculum plans from teachers which would achieve an ethnic diverse curriculum. The decision to incorporate ethnically diverse materials was never an official mandate. Consequently, multi-cultural materials have been added to some parts of the curriculum and then only as supplemental and separate materials.

By making this distinction between multi-culture materials and regular, mainstream curriculum, two things happened: First, the use of multi-cultural curriculum evolved in a random, scattered fashion primarily because the ultimate decision of the use, the quality and type of materials to be used was left up to the discretion of the teacher or on-site school administrator. Some schools used these materials, others did not. Thus, over the last thirty years no uniform formula for multi-culture curriculum was ever developed by the Department of Education at local, state or national level.

Second, by classifying these materials as "supplemental" and offering them as separate topics, multi-culture curriculum never achieved the same status, rank or acceptance of the mainstream curriculum. This approach subtly perpetuated the views of the status quo by reinforcing the notion that only information on White Europeans was worth learning. The very practice of keeping these materials separate implies inferiority, not only of the materials, but of the ethnic groups these materials represent.

Multi-culture curriculum should be totally integrated into the mainstream curriculum and taught even in schools not serving ethnic minority students. This approach will permanently enrich the curriculum for all students and validate the human experience of various ethnic groups who have played significant roles in the development of American society.

In the 21st century it is estimated that 60% of the public school population will be ethnic minorities. In order to effectively teach these children, dramatic changes will have to be made to the curriculum presently utilized in the nation's school system. Educators can begin this process by examining traditionally used materials. Today's curriculum must be reviewed, reassessed and improved.

This entire process requires that educators openly acknowledge the history of racism in American society and the impact of race in education.

Following are suggestions which will aid educators in developing effective multi-culture curriculum:

1. Establish a multi-ethnic curriculum committee to review present curriculum used in the classroom and to monitor curriculum development. This committee can evaluate ethnic information for accuracy, quality, stereotypes. Inaccurate, negative and distorted materials should be replaced

2. Evaluate curriculum to determine that materials relating to ethnically diverse populations are presented in a manner that accurately reflects ethnic diversity
3. Review curriculum to identify cultural assumptions, racism and stereotypes
4. Strive for total integration of multi-culture materials on ethnic groups into main stream curriculum. These materials should not be offered as supplemental materials or separate topics, but should be presented as viable parts of the regular curriculum

****

CURRICULUM DESIGN MODEL

The Curriculum Design Model illustrates the essential components in the curriculum development process. Learning to develop sound curriculum, which will be multi-culture in mature, involves several significant connecting points that enriches the development process. Sound, multi-cultural curriculum is critical in relaying relevant concepts to students and reflects strong: organization, planning and implementation skills.

The Curriculum Design Model arranges the curriculum components in order of stages that curriculum product will evolve. All components are interconnected and progressive. The process begins all over once the cycle is completed.

STAGE 1: Emphasis of instruction of curriculum is the initial stage. Concepts in the curriculum should be presented in a clear, concise manner.

STAGE 2: Identify specific instructional objectives. Instructional objectives must be developed and designed with very specific desired learning outcomes: What is being learned, why it is being learned, the style in which the students will learn most effectively.

STAGE 3: Represents a multiple stage and depends on how successful previous stages 1 & 2 were presented. The degree of success will determine:

    a. Whether or not supplemental materials will be needed or used in the exercise. Additional materials might be needed to adequately meet academic objectives of each student.

    b. The type of activities to use. Students must be able to reiterate the basic skills outlined in the curriculum. Activities developed should focus on basic skills out lined in the curriculum. Activities developed should focus on basic skill content of the curriculum.

STAGE 4: Evaluation of instructional outcomes is the final stage which involves a comprehensive review with students to determine whether or not the curriculum was successful and whether instructional objectives were met. This stage also allows teachers to examine and assess teaching strategies.

The entire process starts again with a new exercise.

THE CURRICULUM DESIGN MODEL

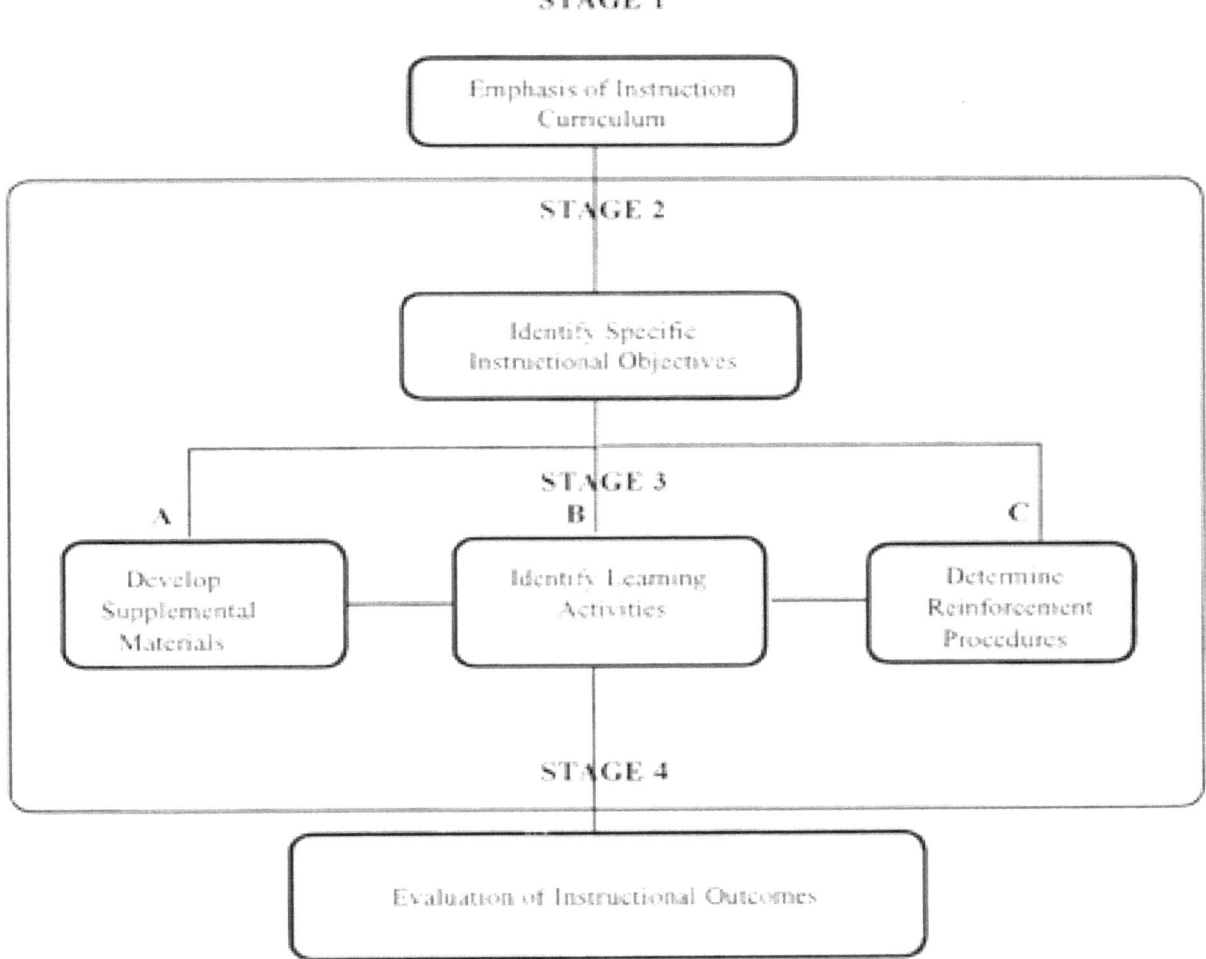

Section VII

Learning Style Assessment Instruments

1. **MULTIDIMENSIONAL INSTRUMENTS:**

Briggs-Myers, Isabel and Briggs, Katherine C. Myers-Briggs Type Indicator. Consulting Psychologists Press, Inc., Palo Alto, CA, (1976).

Description: A measure of personality dispositions and interests based on Jung's theory of types. Suitable for early adolescents through adults. Provides four bipolar scales that can be reported as continuous scores or reduced to types. Requires special training to administer.

Canfield, Albert A. and Canfield, Judith S. Learning Style Inventory, Humanics Media, Ann, Arbor, MI (1976)
Description: Self-report instrument based on a rank ordering of choices for each of thirty questions. For use with junior high and up. Takes about fifteen minutes to administer.

Dunn, Rita, Dunn, Kenneth and Price Gary E. Learning Style Inventory (students, 1978) and Productivity Environmental Preference Survey (adults, 1977), Price Systems, Lawrence, KS.
Description: Self-reported questionnaires yielding information about how a given student learns. There are thirty-six sub-scales covering eighteen elements in four areas: Environmental, emotional, sociological and physical. It is computer scored.

Entwistle, Noel. Short Inventory of Approaches to Studying in Styles of Learning and Teaching. John Wiley & Sons, NY (1981).
Description: A thirty-item test, using a Likert scale, in which students respond to statements concerning their achieving orientation, reproducing orientation, meaning dimension, comprehension style, operation style and versatile approach. An index of learning pathologies can be obtained by summing three sub-scales. There is also

a prediction of success score. Takes about thirty minutes. Appropriate for junior high and up.

Grasha, Anthony F. and Riechmann, Sheryl W. Student Learning Styles, Inst. for Research & Training in Higher Education, Univ of Cinn, OH (1974).
Description: A hand-scored, self-report inventory of ninety items designed to elicit student attitudes toward the courses taken in college or high school and to identify related learning style. Six styles are described: independent, avoidant, collaborative, dependent, competitive and participant.

Hill, Joseph, Cognitive Style Interest Inventory, in Personalized Education Programs Utilizing Cognitive Style Mapping. Oakland Community College, Bloomfield Hills, MI (1971)
Description: A self-report instrument based on a rank ordering that measures abstractions; visual, tactile and auditory perception; motor coordination; and social interaction. Can be used with elementary students and up. Takes appropriately fifty minutes.

Malcom, Paul, Lutz, William, Gerken, Mary and Hoeltke, Gary. Learning Style Identification Scale, Publishers Test Service, Monterey, CA (1981).
Description: A short, 24 item, self-scored rating scale based on the concept of learning style as the "method students use to solve any problem that they encounter in their educational experiences." Five styles are identified based on classification of information, reception and use, cognitive development and self-concept.

Perrin, Janet. Learning Style Inventor: Primary Version. St. John's Univ., NY (1981).
Description: Based on the Learning Style Inventory of Dunn, Dunn and Price and designed for young children. The questionnaire consists of twelve charts, each containing a series of pictures and questions that assesses a different element of learning style. The inventory is individually administered and scored on a student profile form. Takes about twenty minutes.

Ramirez, Manuel and Castaneda, Alfredo. Child Rating Form in Cultural Democracy, Bicognitive, Development and Education, Academic Press, NY (1974)

Description: A direct observation checklist yielding frequency of behavior based on field independence/sensitivity and cultural differences. Teacher rates younger students; older students can rate themselves. Administration time varies. A revised version will soon appear in New Frontiers to be published by Pergamon Press.

Renzulli, Joseph and Smith, Linda. Learning Style Inventory. Creative Learning Press, Conn. (1978)

Description: Both teacher and student forms are available for this sixty-five item instrument designed to measure attitude toward nine modes of instruction. Students and teachers indicate their reasons using a Likert Scale ranging from very unpleasant to very pleasant. Forms are on optical scanning sheets and are scored by computer. Requires thirty minutes to administer and can be used in grades four through twelve.

2.   **COGNITIVE STYLE INSTRUMENTS**

Gardner, R. W., et. al., Transaction Ability Inventory in Cognitive Control: A Study of Individual Consistencies in Cognitive Behavior, Psychological Issues #1, (1959).

Description: Assesses individual variations in memory processing on a continuum of leveling to sharpening. Each subject is asked to judge in inches the size of 150 squares successfully projected on a screen. The squares range in size from one to fourteen inches on a side and are shown in a prescribed order. Levelers are likely to over-generalize, while sharpeners may over-discriminate.

Piaget for Educators. Columbus, OH (1976)

Description: Paper and pencil, group administered tests to reveal formal or concrete operational reasoning. The problems are multiple choice. Torrance, Paul, Reynolds, Cecil R. and Riegel, T.R., **Your Style of Learning and Thinking,** in Gifted Child Quarterly 2, (1977)

Description: No description. pp. 563-73.

Witken, Herman A., **Group Embedded Figures Test** (also Embedded Figures Test and Children's Embedded Figures Test), Psychologists Press, Inc., Palo Alto, CA (1971)
Description: EFT was originally designed for research with the field independent-field dependent aspect of cognitive style and was used to assess analytic ability, social behavior, body concepts, etc. The GEFT is a group version of the test. Field independence and dependence characterize analytical versus global styles of information processing. The latter test takes about fifteen minutes.

3.   **AFFECTIVE STYLE INSTRUMENTS:**

Crandall, V.C., Katkovshy, W., and Crandall, V.J. **Intellectual Achievement Responsibility Questionnaire in Children's Belief in their own Situations**, Child Development 36, (1965)
Description: The IAR Scale is designed to assess internal-external perceptions of the control one exerts specifically in intellectual and academic situation. There are elementary and secondary school versions of the questionnaire.

Hunt, David E., et. al. **Paragraph Completion Method** in Assessing Conceptual Level by Paragraph Completion Method. Ontario Inst. for Studies in Education, (1978)
Description: A semi-projective method to assess the degree of classroom structure needed by students. Conceptual level shown by completing six incomplete statements involving conflict or uncertainty. (1) What I think about rules..., (2) When I am criticize...., (3) What I think about parents..., (4) When someone does not agree with me..., (5) When I am not sure..., (6) When I am told what to do..... Special training required to administer.

Rotter, Julian B., **People in Society (Internal/External) in Generalized Expectations for Internal Versus External Control of Reinforcements**. Psychological Issues 1 (1959)
Description: A questionnaire to find out how people react to certain important events that they experience in their society. Measures the degree of control persons feel over their world.

Wlodkowski, Raymond J., **Student Motivation Information Form**, Univ of Wisc (1978)

Description: A thirty-five item, incomplete sentences test that elicits information about what motivates the person, e.g., intrinsic or extrinsic rewards. Could be administered orally to younger children.

4. **PERCEPTUAL MODALITY INSTRUMENTS:**

Barbe, Walter and Swassing, Raymond. **Swassing-Barbe Modality Index**, Zaner-Bloser (1979)

Description: This is a series of three tasks involving visual, auditory, and kinesthetic-tactile processing of the order of geometric shapes. It can be used with learners of any age but must be individually administered. Results tell the percentage of the time each mode is used successfully. Kit includes a textbook on modality instruction and a filmstrip and tape.

Swassing-Barbe Checklist of Observable Modality Strength Characteristics. This is a one-page brochure for use by teachers as they recall student characteristics.

Barbe, Walter, Find Your Modality Strengths, in Instructor (Jan, 1980)

Description: This is a series of ten incomplete sentences that are suppose to give "a rough idea of the relative strength of each of your modalities." Can be used by teachers and older students.

Mills, Robert. Learning Methods Test. (1955) Available from Mills School

Description: The LMT determines the "students' abilities to learn new words under different teaching procedures. The tasks involve visual, kinesthetic, phonic, and combination presentation of words. Since immediate and delayed recall is assessed, the test takes four days, fifteen minutes each day. It is individually administered.

Reinert, Harry, Edmonds Learning Style Identification Exercise, in One Picture is Worth a Thousand Words? Not necessarily! The Modern Language Journal 60 (1976)

<u>Description:</u> ELSIE provides a profile of students' preferred perceptual styles based on patterns or responses to fifty common English words. Four general categories are defined: visualization, written word (reading), listening, and activity (kinesthetic).

SRI Student Perceiver Interview Guide. Selection Research, Inc., (1978) <u>Description:</u> A structured interview process designed to elicit student perceptions grouped under sixteen themes that are predominantly affective in nature. Institutes leading to trained certification are held regularly in designated cities. Administration time is approximately forty-five minutes. Can be used with intermediate students and up. *Taken from: C. Bennett, "Comprehensive Multi-Cultural Education," 1986

REFERENCES

Baker, Gwendolyn C. Planning and Organizing for Multi-Cultural Instruction. Addison-Wesley Publishing Company. (1983)

Bennett, C. Comprehensive Multi-Cultural Education. Allyn and Bacon, Boston, (1986)

Benson, H. Black Children and Learning Styles. John Hopkins University Press, Baltimore, (1982)

Boykin, A.W. Psychological/Behavioral Serve as a Differentiating Factor in the Task/Academic Performance of Afro-Americans and Whites: Pretheoretical Consideration. Journal of Negro Education (1978)

Case, R. Intellectual Development: Birth to Adulthood. Academic Press, New York (1984)

Cheney, Arnold B. Teaching Children of Different Cultures in the Classroom: A Language Approach. Charles B. Merrill Company, Ohio (1986)

Cole, Brembeck and Walker, Hill, Beginning: Social Affects of Development of Black Children. Cultural Challenge to Education, D.C. Health & Company, Canada. (1973)

Cole, M. Gay J., Glick, J. and Sharp, D.W. The Cultural Context of Learning and Thinking. Basic Books, New York (1971)

Cole, M. and Scribner, S. Culture and Thought. Wiley & Company, (1974)

Cole, M. and Bruner, J. Preliminaries to a Theory of Cultural Differences. National Society for the Study of Education Yearbook, Chicago, (1974)

Dasen, P. Piagetian Psychology: Cross Cultural Contributions. Basic Books, New York, (1977)

Douglas, M. How Institutions Think. Syracuse University Press, Syracuse, NY (1986)

Dunn, R. and Dunn, K. Teaching Students Through Their Individual Learning Styles: A Practical Approach. Reston Publishing Division of Prentice Hall, Reston, VA (1988)

Furth, H. Knowledge is Desire. Columbia University Press, New York (1987)

Glick, J. Culture and Cognition Revisited. In E. Neimark, R. DeLisi and J. Newman (Eds.) Moderators of Competence. Lawrence Erlbaum Publishing, Hillsdale, NJ (1985)

Gollnick, Donna, M. Chinn, and Phillip, C. Multi-Cultural Education in a Pluralistic Society. Third Edition. Merrill Publishing Company, Columbus, OH (1990)

Goodlad, John I., and David, Thomas G. Education and Urban Society. Sage Publication, Inc., California (1984)

Godman, Yetta M. (Ed.) How Children Construct Literacy: Piagetian. International Reading Association (1990).

Hill, J., (et. al) Personalized Education Programs Utilizing Cognitive Learning Styles Mapping. Bloomfield Hills, MI (1971)

Hilliard, Asa. Alternatives to IQ Testing: An approach to the identification of gifted "Minority" children. Final Report to California State Department of Education (1976)

Hunter, William A. Multi-Cultural Education Through Competency Based Teacher Education. American Association of Colleges for Teacher Education, Washington, D.C. (1974)

Irvine, J. Black Students and School Failure: Policies, Practices and Prescription. Greenwood Press, New York (1990)

Karp, I. and Bird, C. Exploration in African System of Thought. Indiana Press, Indiana (1980)

Keefe, J. (Ed.) In Student Learning Styles: Diagnosing and Prescribing Programs. National Association of Secondary School Principles, Reston, VA (1979)

Kirby, P. Cognitive Style and Transfer Skill Acquisition. Information Series No. 195. State University National Center for Research in Vocational Education. Ed. #186685, Columbus, OH

Kolb, D. Disciplinary Inquiry Norms and Students Learning Styles: Diverse Pathways for Growth In the Modern American College. Arthur Chickering (1981)

Lesser, G., Fifer, G. and Clark, D. Mental Abilities of Children from Different Social Class and Cultural Groups. University of Chicago Press for the Society of Research in Child Development, Chicago (1964)

Miller-Jones, D. Differences in social and cognitive information processing between high and low achieving five year old Black children. In J. McAdoo and W. Cross (Eds.) Proceedings of the Fifth Conference on Empirical Research in Black Psychology. Africana Studies & Research Center, Cornell University Press and NIMH, New York (1981)

Neimark, D. and DeLisi, R. Moderator of Competence, Newman, Hillsdale, NJ (1988)

Ramirez, M. III and Castaneda, A. Cultural Democracy, Bi-Cognitive Development and Education. Academic Press, New York (1974)

Rebok, G. Life Span Cognitive Development. Holt, Rinehart and Winston, New York (1987)

Shale, S. Culture, Style and the Education Process. Charles C. Thomas Publisher, Springfield, IL (1989)

Sigel, I.E. Language of the Disadvantaged: The Distancing Hypothesis. In C. S. Lavatelli (Ed.) <u>Language Training in Early Childhood Education</u>. University of Illinois Press, Urbana (1971)

Singer, Robert N. and Richard F. Gerson, "Learning Strategies, Cognitive Processes and Motor Learning (1985)

Simmons, W. The Role of Cultural Salience in Ethnic and Social Class Differences in Cognitive Performance. <u>Fourth Conference on Empirical Research in Black Psychology.</u> Africana Studies and Research Center, Cornell University, NY (1979)

Spindler, George Dearborn. <u>Education and Cultural Process: Anthropological Approaches.</u> 2nd Edition, Waveland Press, Stanford University, CA (1987)

Strike, C. <u>Black Students in Higher Education</u>. Southern Illinois University Press, Chicago (1987)

Ward, M. <u>Them Children</u>. Waveland Press, (Holt, Rinehart and Winston), New York (1986)

Watkin, Herman A. <u>Cognitive Style in Academic Performance and in Teacher-Student Relations.</u> In Individuality in Learning. Samuel Messick & Associates (Eds.) Jossey-Bass, San Francisco (1976)

****

NOTES

TEACHER AWARENESS/ASSESSMENT INSTRUMENT

Accurate observation is a critical variable in developing specific techniques and strategies to work with African American children effectively. Diagnosing a student's academic potential is intricately tied to the teacher's understanding of learning styles and social behavior.

This workshop manual includes two specific diagnostic tools to assist teachers to better perform their teaching responsibility in working with African American children. These diagnostic tools will assist teachers in becoming sensitive to the way they perform as teachers and sensitive to the way African American students learn.

Research shows that the perceptions and attitudes of a teacher toward the learner will ultimately affect a teacher's attitude and behavior in the classroom. This teacher assessment instrument is an individual teaching tool designed to enable teachers to explore their own beliefs, attitudes and feelings regarding their African American students.

This instrument can provide invaluable information on how teachers may view the Black culture and introspectively allow teachers to privately examine their own knowledge about themselves and their skills to effectively teach African American children.

Teaching African American children effectively requires that teachers have an accurate assessment of the culture from which these children come. This will enhance the teacher's ability to plan constructive curriculum and effective lesson plans to increase learning for African American children.

The instrument addresses eight distinct areas that are critical in understanding the culture of these students. Following is a list of specific objectives of the teacher assessment instrument:

SCORING
The scoring of the instrument consist of a range score

1. To examine and measure a teacher's knowledge of African American culture.
2. To illustrate specific areas that are critical to understanding African American children.
3. To examine a teacher's attitude toward African American children.
4. To examine a teacher's sensitivity regarding working with African American children.
5. To examine a teacher's cultural awareness regarding African American culture.

of 1-5, with 5 being high. A score of 5 would indicate that the individual is culturally aware and sensitive to the needs, culture and academic potential of African American children. This individual should be effective in working with African American children.

A score 3-4 would illustrate that the individual requires additional training in terms of cross-cultural communication, the impact of culture on the learning process and how to teach effectively cross culturally. These individuals should consider taking additional course work on learning styles and working with culturally diverse students.

A score of 1-2 illustrates that this individual lacks the understanding, awareness of African American children, the culture of these children and their academic ability/potential. Work needs to be done in acquiring a better understanding of how African American children learn, the culture of these children and their academic ability/potential.

TEACHER AWARENESS/ASSESSMENT INSTRUMENT

Name: _____	Date: _____
Oberserver: _____	Grade Level: _____

Code: Select a number from 1-5 which most closely reflects your view:

1. Not True 2. Seldom True 3. Sometimes True 4. Often True 5. Almost Always True

TEACHING STYLE/BEHAVIOR	CODE
CULTURAL VALUES	
1. I am aware of how students feel about their culture.	
2. I understand the culture of African American children and of children from the dominant culture.	
3. I am aware of the values associated with the African American culture.	
4. I am aware of the imposition of values in the classroom.	
ENVIRONMENTAL EXPOSURE	
1. I understand the positive feature of the African American culture.	
2. I do not consciously penalize African American children from impoverished environments.	
3. I do not view the environment of African American children as inferior.	
4. I understand the impact environmental factors have on the learning process.	
SOCIAL CLASS	
1. I understand the positive features of the African American culture.	
2. I understand the differences in social class when working with African American children and children from other social class groups.	
3. In classroom situations, I do not consciously devalue the social class of children which might be different from my own.	
4. I try very hard to make children from low socio-economic groups feel comfortable and positive about themselves.	
TOTAL LIFE EXPERIENCE	
1. I am not judgmental when relating to children whose total life experience is different from my own.	
2. I try very hard to help my students find and identify positive aspects of their life experiences and to share these experiences with their classmates.	
3. I understand the importance of ethnicity and try to incorporate ethnic diversity in the classroom.	
4. I do not view students with a different total life experience as inferior.	

SELF-IMAGE	
1. I understand when African American children have a positive self-image.	
2. I consider cultural differences when defining the self-image of my students.	
3. I understand the importance of a positive self-image for African American students.	
4. I understand the harmful effects of a negative self-image in the learning situation, especially when it comes to teaching African American students.	
PEER/TEACHER RELATIONSHIPS	
1. I understand how African American children feel about peer relationships.	
2. I understand the impact of a positive relationship with African American children in terms of motivation and learning.	
3. I understand how African American children react to me as a teacher.	
4. I do not grade African American children on how they relate to me as a teacher.	
LOCUS OF CONTROL	
1. I understand what type of stimuli is most effective in enhancing the learning environment for African American children.	
2. I make an effort to match curriculum with the learning styles of African American students.	
3. I am not judgmental in my expectations of African American students.	
4. I am innovative and creative in integrating the life experience of my African American students in the classroom situation.	
PERCEPTIONS	
1. I work very hard to understand how African American children in my class perceive themselves in relation to other students.	
2. I do not grade African American students on how well they like or dislike me as a teacher.	
3. I understand the importance of perceptions as an important variable in the learning process.	
4. I do not react negatively or in a judgmental manner toward African American students if their perception of the world and reality is extremely different from my own.	

PLEASE FILL IN THE BLANKS:

1. One of the most serious problems facing the school system is _____

2. The curriculum is _____

3. Parents are _____

4. Administrators are _____

5. Teachers are _____

6. Students are _____

THE BLACK STUDENT OBSERVATIONAL BEHAVIORAL ASSESSMENT INSTRUMENT

This instrument is designed to assess the overall preferred learning style or model of functioning of Black children. The instrument will allow teachers to determine what curriculum plan to use to enhance learning for these students.

The instrument is used to facilitate observing and coding learning behavior and social interaction of Black students in the classroom, applying information contained in the Black Socio- Cultural Cognitive Learning Style Matrix Model.

Teachers should be able to code the number and percentage of cognitive/affective skills being displayed by Black students. This will assist teachers to plan effective and meaningful curriculum activities, thereby enhancing the learning process for Black students.

This instrument is based on the conceptual Matrix Model of the Black Socio-Cultural Cognitive Learning Style. Specific content items are designed from each variable that constitutes the model.

Teachers utilizing this instrument will be able to identify strengths that Black children bring with them in the teaching/learning environment. Thus, enabling them to design more effective lesson plans for these students. Specific objectives of the instrument include:

o Identifying the learning style of Black students.

o Identifying strengths.

o Identifying conditions under which Black students learn best.

o Identifying preferred mode of learning.

o Developing a realistic profile of Black students.

o Identifying achievement potential of Black students.

SCORING

The scoring of the instrument consist of a range score of 1-5 with 5 and 4 being the highest scores that can be obtained. A high score on this instrument illustrates a person's level of understanding of each test item.

The highest score on each questions suggests that an individual does not need to work on a particular area and should be effective in planning instructional activities for Black students.

A mid-range score of 3 indicates that the individual may not be clear on their understanding of a specific area and should enroll in professional development courses and workshops on learning styles in order to gain a more comprehensive view of the lifestyle and culture of Black children. This will enable them to design and develop meaningful instructional lesson plans for these students.

Low scores of 1-2, indicates that the individual lacks a clear understanding, awareness or knowledge of the test items. A low score suggests that an individual has little content knowledge of a particular area and needs professional training to develop effective observational skills to assist them in understanding the learning ability and potential of Black children.

Keep in mind that the scoring process if very subjective, but it is designed to train teachers to work effectively with Black students. In order for this instrument to be useful, teachers should be objective and open during this self-evaluation process. It is hoped that this exercise will provide teachers with a comprehensive view of their skills in terms of being culturally aware, sensitive and observance. This should greatly enhance their effectiveness in working with Black students.

THE BLACK SOCIO-CULTURAL COGNITIVE LEARNING STYLE

BLACK STUDENT OBSERVATIONAL/ASSESSMENT INSTRUMENT

Name: _____ Date: _____

Oberserver: _____ Grade Level: _____

Code: Select a number from 1-5 which most closely reflects your view.
1. Not True 2. Seldom True 3. Sometimes True 4. Often True 5. Almost Always True

BLACK STUDENT BEHAVIOR	CODE SELECTED
EXTENDED FAMILY RELATIONS	
1. Understands the importance of each student being an important member of the classroom setting.	
2. Exhibits signs of being responsible in the learning situation.	
3. Exhibits the ability to adjust easily to changes which occurs in the learning environment.	
4. Exhibits signs of being able to adjust to various role models in the teaching/ learning situation.	
5. Exhibits signs of being aware of authority figures in the learning situation.	
6. Exhibits signs of being able to understand clearly defined roles in the learning situation.	
CULTURAL RESILIENCY	
1. Exhibits the ability to be consciously aware of racial differences of others in the classroom environment.	
2. Exhibits the ability to be conscious of the differences in social class of others in the classroom environment.	
3. Exhibits the ability to effectively deal with value conflict in the classroom environment.	
4. Is aware of racial distinctions made in American society.	
5. Exhibits a positive self-image regarding racial identity.	
6. Responds in a positive way during discussions and activities involving race, culture group and social class.	

CULTURAL CREATIVITY	
1. Exhibits signs of creative expressions in the learning situation.	
2. Exhibits problem-solving ability in the learning situation.	
3. Exhibits strong observational skills in the teaching/learning situation.	
4. Exhibits the ability to memorize and translate information easily.	
5. Exhibits the ability to improvise when completing classroom assignments, working with others and working on assignments that requires imagination.	
6. Seems to enjoy creative projects.	

GROUP ORIENTATION	
1. Exhibits the ability to form close relationships with peers and others. 2. Appears to be empathetic toward other classmates and teachers.	
3. Able to make distinctions and develop strategies in solving problems.	
4. Is flexible in adjusting to new situations in the classroom environment.	
5. Not afraid to take on tasks in the learning situation.	
6. Exhibits analytical skills in the teaching/learning situation.	

HIGHLY DEVELOPED MOTOR SKILLS	
1. Exhibits strong physical skills in play activities.	
2. Has the ability to perform complex motor skills.	
3. Exhibits creative skills in play activities.	
4. Enjoys being able to engage in physical games.	
5. Able to conceptualize complex physical movement easily.	
6. Exhibits analogical/propositional skills in the learning situation.	

EARLY MATURATION (INDEPENDENT LEARNER)	
1. Is an active participant in classroom activities.	
2. Able to respond in a mature manner to classroom assignments and responsibilities.	
3. Seems to adjust well to changes in the classroom situation.	
4. Is very cooperative, rather than competitive, when working in teams.	
5. Exhibits risk-taking behavior when encountering new activities in the classroom environment.	
6. Able to work independently of others and displays a sense of self-control.	

BI DIALECTIC LANGUAGE PATTERNS	
1. Occasionally uses a non-standard language pattern in verbal expressions and communications.	
2. Has the ability to adequately define unfamiliar words.	
3. Exhibits standard formal language patterns in verbal expressions and communications.	
4. Makes adequate use of bio-dialectic language patterns in processing information, either verbally or in writing.	
5. Exhibits the ability to appropriately substitute non-standard language when translating classroom instructions or when responding verbally.	
6. Exhibits a broad vocabulary of non-standard language terms and phrases.	

ENVIRONMENTAL AUTONOMY	
1. Exhibits the ability to make choices easily in the learning situation.	
2. Appears to be very flexible when interacting with others in the classroom environment.	
3. Exhibits the ability to work independently and make decisions about classroom work.	
4. Able to resolve conflict successfully without any outside interference.	
5. Able to follow directions and complete assigned tasks.	
6. Appears to be very self-reliant and dependable.	

COMMENTS:

The Black Socio-Cultural Cognitive Learning Style Training Manual is an innovative way to successfully teach African American students in the classroom. This model has been used in classrooms throughout the nation for the past twenty-five years. Although the model has been updated over the ears to ensure releveance, the principles, strategies, techniques and philosophical structure of the model has remained the same.

The foundation of the Black Socio-Cultural Cognitive Learning Style is that African American childer can achieve academically as well as any other student in a culturally enriched learning environment taught by culturally proficient and competent teachers.

The Black Socio-Cultural Cognitive Learning Style Model is a training tool for teachers and education seeking to become more culturally competent and proficient in working with African American learners. The following products focus on:

- Ethnic diversity

- African American culture

- How to teach effectively to African American learners.

- Cultural awareness

- Cultural proficiency and cultural competency

- Cognition and cognitive development

- Learning styles

- Teaching styles

Dr. Isaiah Sessoms

Executive Director, ESR, Inc.